WITHDRAWN

THE
BURNING GLASS

A PLAY

by

CHARLES MORGAN

With a Preface

ON POWER OVER NATURE

LONDON
MACMILLAN & CO LTD
NEW YORK · ST MARTIN'S PRESS
1953

*This book is copyright in all countries which
are signatories to the Berne Convention*

MACMILLAN AND COMPANY LIMITED
London Bombay Calcutta Madras Melbourne

THE MACMILLAN COMPANY OF CANADA LIMITED
Toronto

ST MARTIN'S PRESS INC
New York

PR
6025
O 645B8

PRINTED IN GREAT BRITAIN

POSTSCRIPT

THE title of my play arose so naturally from its subject that its clash with Mr. Walter de la Mare's *The Burning-Glass and Other Poems* did not enter my mind until the eleventh hour. His good-will in then bidding me go forward enables me to add my gratitude to my apologies.

C. M.

PREFACE

ON POWER OVER NATURE

I

The Burning Glass is neither a debate nor an allegory, but a straightforward story of men and women facing a crisis in their lives. It pleads no cause. Nevertheless it indicates a point of view, and if it should lead out a spectator's or a reader's thought beyond the frontiers of its visible action, I shall be rewarded, as any story-teller is, beside the nursery fire, when (and only when) his audience forget him and begin to imagine for themselves.

The tale had its origin in my belief that humanity is threatened by a change — let us call it a subversion of the natural order — different not only in degree but in kind from any change that it has undergone since man became distinct from the beasts. This belief is part of a larger theme which has engaged my mind for many years. 'Our fight', Professor Butterfield lately wrote,[1] 'is against some devilry that lies in the very process of things, against something that we might even call daemonic forces existing in the air. The forces get men into their grip, so that the men themselves are victims in a sense, even if it is by

---

[1] *Christianity in European History*, by Herbert Butterfield, M.A., Professor of Modern History in the University of Cambridge (London: Collins, 1952).

some fault in their own nature — they are victims of a sort of possession.' That the fight should be described in these terms, not by a priest, a poet or a story-teller but by a Cambridge historian of the first rank, is a sign of the times, for the nature of the struggle is not to be understood unless we understand that it is a part of history itself, underlying the lesser struggles which we call economic or dynastic. But the daemonic forces vary their strategy from age to age ; they attack us through the fashions of our thought ; and it was one of these infiltrations into our defences — which may make men the 'victims of a sort of possession' — that I discussed in an earlier essay on 'Mind Control'.[1] The vulnerable point indicated in *The Burning Glass* is the long-prevalent fashion of believing, uncritically, that each development of man's power over Nature, unless it happens to threaten his body with injury or death, is necessarily beneficent. This great lie has given the daemonic forces their modern opportunity. The material changes experienced by man hitherto have been biological, social, political, economic ; or scientific in the sense of his having, step by step and always in his proportion as a created being, wrung from a seemingly reluctant Nature small extensions of her licence to him. The change now threatening him, the subversion of the natural order to which he is already deeply though not finally committed, appears to underlie all these.

Hitherto his revolutions, conducted under Nature's sometimes compassionate, always ironic, eye, have busied themselves about what were, from Nature's point of view,

[1] *Liberties of the Mind*, by Charles Morgan (London : Macmillan, 1951).

trivial questions. How, during his brief tenancy, should he persuade his little plot, the Earth, to yield him the wherewithal to exist? With what tools should he culti-vate it? Should he carry his loads on his back, or drag them on a sledge or put them on wheels? How fast should the wheels go round? Who should control each patch of Earth, he or his neighbour? How should its product be distributed? Sometimes, in religious mood, he fought a war to decide which gods should be asked to propitiate Nature so that she might grant him more or less sun, more or less rain, and perhaps a few extra months in which to enjoy the grape.

Always — except when he contemplated another life than this — what he struggled for was a slightly longer and less onerous tenancy of his Earth-plot; and though his struggle was often heroically defiant, it was at root humble. Fighting Nature, he knew himself outmatched. It did not occur to him that she, the mighty, the powerful, the enduring, the stubborn, would ever abdicate in favour of his pygmy self. Therefore he did not ask how he would live if she gave signs of doing so, or whether, if he were exempted from her tutelage and invested with her powers, he was fit to live at all. Nor did he ask how such a change in his relationship with Nature might affect his relationship with his God or his Devil.

These questions are now presenting themselves to physicists and philosophers, and, I think, at varying levels of consciousness, to a great part of mankind. They present themselves urgently, in *The Burning Glass*, to Christopher Terriford and, through him, to others. But the play does not attempt to advance a solution of the underlying problem — only to illustrate it in the particular instance of these men and women at grips with it; for, unlike the social and political problems to which we are accustomed on platform and stage, a new dispensation of Nature (if that is what faces us) is not a subject for debate terminable by closure and vote.

The idea is as yet too unfamiliar. Common revolutions we know; periodically they dispute the rule of the roost, but at least they presuppose the continuance of the farmyard. A subversion of the relationship between man and Nature does not presuppose the continuance of anything we have known on earth. The idea of it has to be apprehended as poetry is, or felt as we feel, with leaping imagination, a touch in the dark. For that reason I have tried to tell my story in such a way that an audience, listening to it for its own sake and forgetting the storyteller, may discover for themselves strange faces in the fire, and perhaps see through and beyond these faces before it is time for all of us now living to go to bed.

2

I shall try, therefore, even in this preface, to come as little as I can between the reader and the persons of my play. A dramatist must know much more of the thought, the antecedents and, perhaps, the future of his characters than is directly told on the stage, for he has lived with them before their entrances, pursued them beyond their exits, and been inside their heads. He must not always be inside their heads; if he assume the godlike privilege of omniscience, he will find — to the ruin of his play — that his will, not theirs, is done. They

must have the liberty of his most intimate friends to
surprise him in speech, action and thought; they must
have their secrets from him lest his curiosity, and his
story, die. And yet they are, in the most profoundly
imaginative sense, his intimates. They have contributed
to his thought as he to theirs. If he wishes to pursue,
beyond the boundaries of the stage, a theme that has
been illustrated in their lives, he probably does well
not to discuss it *ex cathedra* but to see it in the light
of their fallibility, which may usefully remind him of
his own.

And, of course, one is inclined to add, it would be for
him a happy privilege if, instead of being separated from
them in his own home, he were an inhabitant of theirs;
if, before the play began, he had been their guest at
Terriford House, and, now that the play is done, could
still visit them there and talk with them of what is past,
and of what is to come. This privilege is, in a sense,
mine. Christopher Terriford, his friends and his enemy,
have no 'originals' in my acquaintance, and certainly the
Prime Minister they knew, Mr. Montagu Winthrop, is
not to be found in Downing Street; but by fortunate
chance, I write this preface in the room where, last
winter, the play was begun and for the most part written,
and this room, with a slight change of compass bearing,
a shift of the fireplace and an added door to the garden,
is uncommonly like the South Room at Terriford House.
If I were to leave my table and plant myself with my back
to the actual fireplace, I should have my back to the
audience too, and should face the triple-windowed bay
through which Hardlip looked in one morning in the

small hours. At one end of this long room stands the door by which Tony Lack would start on his way to the Experimental Unit or, upstairs, to bed; at the other end is another door, leading through an ante-room and hall, to the main entrance. Mary Terriford's piano is in its place, bearing Nelson in bronze. Even the chess-table is here, which, throughout those wintry months, while flaring logs threw their light across its squares, insisted on becoming a principal actor in the play.

The familiarity, I would almost say the domesticity, of the chess-table is relevant, because the Terrifords' South Room, though for a little while invaded by violent events foreign to its character, was in essence domestic, and the chess-table, at which Christopher and Mary played their game every night, was part of its custom. For several generations before Christopher's birth the South Room had been the casual meeting-place of the family, where they read or wrote or played chess if they had no ardent wish to be alone, where they talked or didn't talk as they pleased. It was an unself-conscious, undemanding, good-humoured room which had learned in the course of time that the Terrifords and their ladies belonged, or firmly believed they belonged, to a world that, for all its changes and chances, was unlikely to go mad. The laws of gravity would not slip into reverse and the carpet rise up against them. Their looking-glass would not turn over-night into a distorting mirror. Any one of them might, if he had imagination enough in poetry or physics or faith, walk through a looking-glass and bring back news from the other side; but he would bring it back quietly, and take his glass of sherry in the

South Room without supposing that he was the Red Queen or the White Knight. The Terrifords, when they dreamed dreams, seldom entered the dimension of nightmare, and never stayed in it.

3

This may explain — though it will not excuse to a strictly logical mind — an inconsistency in Christopher Terriford. Why, if he was quick to grasp the implications of his discovery of the Burning Glass, had he not seen long ago that his work on Weather Control was open to the same criticism? Why had he always thought of Weather Control as 'beneficent' or 'harmless enough', and failed to understand that, if ever it became operative, it might produce a major distortion of the natural order?

The general answer is that when our conscience fords a river it ordinarily requires, unless the angels carry it, more than one intellectual stepping-stone; and the particular answer, in Christopher Terriford's case, is that by temperament and training he was disinclined to take an alarmist view of anything — least of all, of those matters which, like his own and his father's experimental work, were part of his daily life. It was his habit to keep his head, not to dramatize himself or his job, and to ride his imagination on the curb.

He had had misgivings about Weather Control, but they had been for the most part practical and even humorous. His father, Sir George Terriford, had chuckled from time to time at the thought that a Government department, given a chance to regulate the weather,

would make a worse fist of it than 'the wayward Clerk',
and had smiled at the prospect of setting diplomacy by
the ears. There would, he foresaw, be teething troubles
of administration if he ever carried his experiments
beyond the laboratory stage and found an effective way
of using the particles of the upper atmosphere as a means
of influencing climate. But that had not been for him a
reason to hesitate. Two decades of his life had been spent
in the nineteenth century — long enough for him, who
played with black kittens, and marched up mountains, and
went to church on Sunday mornings, to have absorbed
the self-confidence of its scientific tradition. Men — and
politicians in particular — were often blunderers. That
was because they were swayed by wild-cat ideas, as men
with a scientific training were not. Their idealism had
its head in the air and their scepticism buried its head in
the ground. Naturally, when they were asked to use the
gifts of science, they misused them at first; hence the
political, economic and social difficulties that had accom-
panied the Industrial Revolution. 'But you wouldn't go
back on the Industrial Revolution, would you?' Men
corrected their mistakes in the end. They blundered, but
they weren't knaves or fools. To suppose that they
were was to give the Devil the key to your nursery.
'And anyhow,' George Terriford would say, 'science,
not the use of it, is our job. We have to bring home the
toy; someone else must teach the children how to play
with it.' The idea that the Devil might be in the toy did
not enter his head.

Nor, while his concern was with Weather Control, did
it enter Christopher's.

When atomic energy was let out of the box, only a
few were stricken with horror at the thing itself, as
distinct from the bomb that was its incidental product.
The general response was wonder, even proud wonder,
at the prodigy, and horror at its destructive power. This
was extremely human. At any manifestation of new
power in their own hands — the first train, the first
flying-machine, presumably the first wheel — men leap
with pride and wonder. Next, they ask whether it will
hurt their bodies. Even to-day, when there is talk of
journeying to Mars, discussion is of how to get there
and of what new powers or riches we may bring back :
few ask whether it is in the proportion of our lives, still
fewer whether it is within the province of the human
spirit, to undertake such a journey, to rape such powers.
We behave in these great matters as a boy behaves
towards his first bicycle. So for the most part the world
is still behaving towards atomic energy, asking only how
to control its warlike and develop its 'beneficent' uses —
in brief, how to ride the bicycle without falling off it.

But there are some who have begun to suspect that
atomism differs from bicycling not only in degree but in
kind, that we are passing into a new category of power,
and that not our bodies only are threatened. The
problem may no longer be the technical one of learning
how to ride, how to play with the toy ; it may be the
much older problem, familiar to Adam and Prometheus,
of learning how not to blaspheme. This aspect of the
matter presented itself to Christopher Terriford when he

discovered the Burning Glass — but presented itself, at first, only in an intuitive shrinking, which he was inclined to discount as superstitious; as the modern world, schooled in rationalism, is inclined to discount its own increasing monitions of poison at the source of its powers. Only when time had passed did Christopher attain a firm and reasoned assurance of evil intrinsic in the Burning Glass itself.

This appeared to him fully as a result of his trying to explain to his wife, Mary, and his mother, Lady Terriford, what had happened. They already knew that the electro-magnetic waves, called Terriford waves, which had earned his honours for Christopher's father, were controlled by certain instruments of which the latest — Christopher's own — was Machine Six. The purpose of the machine was to use the ionized particles of the upper atmosphere in a new way. They were already used as reflectors of certain wireless impulses. The Terriford machine would use them as lenses interposed between the sun and the earth. If this could be done, if the ionized particles could be polarized or orientated into a lens-like pattern, the sun's rays might be 'focused' in such a way as to increase or diminish their local power on the earth's surface and even to affect the formation and the precipitation of cloud — in brief, to influence sunshine and rainfall.

The theory had been carried far in Sir George Terriford's day; the connexion between light and ionization had been steadily and deeply investigated; and Christopher was at least certain that no principle would emerge to forbid the development of lens-like patterns in the upper atmosphere. Indeed they had been formed and had produced measurable effects on temperature and humidity; but these effects, though Machine Six was able to localize them accurately, were so feeble that the Terriford system had remained in the laboratory stage.

There were two reasons for this: first, that the 'lens-like' pattern was, or had been, imperfect — too little like a lens; second, and now the more important, that it was 'held wrong'. Christopher explained this to Lady Terriford and Mary by taking them into the garden with a large magnifying glass in his hand. The sun was shining but heavy rain had recently fallen and the ground was wet. When he held the magnifying glass so that the sun fell through it on to the lawn, the effect at first was a widely diffused area of increased illumination, but, within the area, no remarkable increase of heat: the lens was being 'held wrong'. But, as he manipulated the glass, the area of illumination shrank and the intensity increased until at last the sun's rays were focused on a circle with a diameter of half an inch, not golden but white; and when this circle was directed on to a fallen leaf it burned a hole in the leaf, and when it was turned on to a wet plantain, the plantain began at once to smoulder, little columns of smoke arose from it, it crackled and was burned out: the lens was being 'held right'. What had happened, Christopher said, was that he had hit upon a setting of Machine Six which gave this result. All he had ever hoped for was that Machine Six might learn 'to hold the lens a bit less vaguely' and that gradually it would enable him to contract the area of warmth. Now, jumping all the intermediate stages, he had hit upon a setting that 'makes the daisies sizzle. . . . And that daisy,' he said, looking at the blackened remains, 'is New York or Moscow or London, or where you will.'

Lady Terriford saw it as an achievement, a step forward in the continuous march of Progress. 'Your dear father,' she said, 'would have been very proud.'

Mary was silent for a little while before she spoke: 'Twice, Christopher, you said you "*hit upon*" the Burning Glass setting. What did you mean?'

'Just that.'

'Just chance?'

'In so far as anything is "just chance". In fact, nothing is.'

'You mean you didn't calculate it?'

Christopher hesitated. 'No,' he said, 'I didn't. And yet, if calculation on those lines hadn't been my meat and drink for years, the thing wouldn't have come. It was what my father used to call "a jump". They happen sometimes in mathematics and physics. You get the result, so to speak, without following the steps. You arrive first and look back for the reasons afterwards.'

'But not a fluke?' Mary asked.

'By no means.'

'Nor a guess?'

'N-no.'

'What, then?'

'A suddenness,' Christopher answered. 'Total. Certain. Beyond reason. Like a line of poetry to Keats. Like falling in love.'

Days passed. It became evident to Mary that he was deeply troubled. Even their chess broke down; he was playing like a fool. To her questions, he would at first answer only that he was uncertain what to do with the Burning Glass, how to develop and apply it. Then at last he said : 'I told you that my coming on the setting was one of my father's "jumps". I told you, didn't I, it was like what I imagine the coming of a supreme line must be to a poet ? Or like falling in love ? . . . Sudden. Complete. . . . So it was, in its suddenness and completeness. . . . But this was different. This wasn't happiness. This was — quite filthily unpleasant, as if . . .'

Mary had listened intently when he had first described his experience ; she listened more intently now. It had seemed to her that, at the outset, he had been describing what was in essence a religious experience. The 'jump' of the man of science, the poet's flash, the uncalculating self-loss for which his shorthand has been the phrase, 'falling in love', were all, in their suddenness, their completeness, their transcendence of reason, visionary ; they were, in their nature, conversions. Now, to give him time, she spoke of this. He listened silently until she used the word : 'Conversion'. Then he said : 'It felt like the opposite. . . .'

'You know, Mary,' he continued, 'it was very odd. I have made "jumps" before — not like this one, but small jumps ; mathematicians do. It has always been a tremendously exciting experience but a happy one, like coming out of a tangled wood into sunshine on an open mountain-side. This time what I came out into wasn't light but——'

He broke off again ; then, putting an arm in hers and holding fast, he went on : 'Or put it this way. Each time, the jump has meant for me quite simply that, instead of climbing a ladder rather laboriously step by step, I have been suddenly promoted a dozen rungs, and have rubbed my eyes a bit and been surprised and delighted to find myself there. It has been all *right*; the ladder has been the same ladder, part of the same natural order in which I was before the jump. But this time it was different. It didn't feel like order; it felt like chaos. The ladder wasn't there. Even now, though I have the setting, I can't work back from it. I don't like it.'

'Then,' she said, 'why don't you let it go?'

'You mean, forget it? Never communicate it to any-one? No man of science has ever killed power. Can I do that?'

'If it is devilish,' she said, 'you have to.'

5

The word 'devilish' was not an easy one to him. He and she used the same language of thought, but not always the same vocabulary; she passing with rare directness through the symbol to the reality, he remaining aware of the symbol He was intellectually shy of her simplicities, of her use of the words of her childhood (that was to say, of the Bible) as short-cuts to meaning. Nevertheless he knew, because he loved her, when she was a step ahead of him; and that evening, in the South Room, it was a Bible that he put over her shoulder and spread upon her lap. It lay open at the fourth chapter of Luke and he ran his finger down the margin of the first eight verses.[1]

'That is what you meant.'

[1] The Authorized Version; others differ.

She read, then turned, but he was gone, and when he came into the room again and sat down at the chess-table she, because she loved him and knew that he was no longer a step behind, did not speak of the verses.

6

The battle which Christopher fought during the weeks before he allowed the Prime Minister to be invited to Terriford House had three phases : in the first, he hankered after the simplicity of destroying all memory of his discovery ; in the second, he was tempted by the hope of precluding its military use and allowing its 'peaceful' uses ; in the third, he adopted the opposite policy of forbidding all uses except, in certain circumstances, the military. This decision underlies the play itself.

The first phase, upon which the others depended, required of him a revolution in his thought. The old high tradition of scientific research, which he had been brought up to love and honour, presupposed a community of knowledge to which you freely contributed your results. Research was an end in itself, no more associated in his mind with ideas of power or wealth or secrecy than song is associated with these ideas in the mind of a blackbird. What he would normally have done with any discovery of his was to publish it.

The Burning Glass had given the lie to this principle. It was true that the instant excitement of discovery had sent him running from the Unit, as a child runs home with its prize, to tell his wife, his mother and Tony Lack of the effect he had obtained, but he had told no one how to obtain the effect. On the contrary, he had broken up the setting on Machine Six so that no mind but his should possess it. That he — he of all men — should have been swept by this passionate impulse to conceal, was a shock to him.

He could afterwards give himself reasons for concealment. Whatever else the Burning Glass might become, it was evidently a military weapon that must not be put into enemy hands. But this argument of discretion had come later; his impulse to conceal had been urgent and intuitive. It was the enormity of the thing itself that had warned him to hide it, his sense of its being monstrous and corrupt, a leprosy on Nature's face.

This idea of there being the Devil in his toy was one to which Christopher was drawn back again and again, but his well-balanced and unextreme mind fought against it as the mind of the world has fought against the idea of there being anything inherently daemonic in atomic energy. He asked himself, as the world asks itself in the atomic context, whether it might not be right to find a way, if a way could be found, to withhold the military use of the Burning Glass but to make other uses of it available. At the moment this was impracticable. Just as nuclear physicists had arrived at an extreme or 'explosive' use of atomic energy while a moderate and controlled use of it was still beyond their reach, so had he 'jumped' to an extreme effect from which as yet he could not work back; the horses of the sun, which he knew how to release on earth, were by no means his tame creatures to ride or drive. But that, he thought, would come in the end. In time, he or someone else would harness them.

For a moment, he saw this as a benefaction to mankind, as, no doubt, in the Garden, Eve saw the apple. Would there not be Weather Control, which he had always desired, to give all men the fruits of the earth in undue season ? Would there not be an infinite supply of pure heat to drive all the machines of the world ? . . . And the devil, taking him up into an high mountain, shewed unto him all the kingdoms of the world in a moment of time. And the devil said unto him, All this power will I give thee. . . . And Jesus answered and said unto him, Get thee behind me, Satan.

But his silent memory of the verses was not enough to quiet his mind. He went to Mary and said : 'Read me the verses I showed you.' She found them and laid the Bible upon his knee as he had laid it upon her lap.

'No,' he said, 'read them aloud to me ; I want to hear your voice in them.' And she read them peacefully.

7

It became clear to him then that the development of man's power over Nature, which the last decades had witnessed, implied a subversion of the natural order, and that to regard this subversion as 'devilish' was not superstitious but reasonable.

The use or avoidance of the word, he reflected, is a matter of fashion ; therefore of small account. We waste our time in arguing that there is no Satan if we acknowledge a satanic principle and design. Indeed, it may be a part of that design to conceal itself from men by persuading them to abandon the anthropomorphic name which their forefathers used to intimate the principle. It is one thing, and no doubt a proud and subtle thing, to repel philosophical error ; it is another, and a simpler, to say, Get thee behind me, Satan. The dire name and the words of Jesus himself may be no more than shorthand for the truth. Very well, but they are a shorthand which we children have learned to read. Let us use the great words still — God, Satan ; heaven, hell — lest, for want of them, we babble arrogantly of our toys.

We may say then (according to the fashion of our language) of the power-predicament in which the human race finds itself, either that it is a trap laid for us with satanic guile or that it has arisen from two centuries of history in which evil has been accumulating under cover of good. Tennyson, in his prophetic mood, was not unaware—

> Are God and Nature then at strife,
> That Nature lends such evil dreams ?

— but for most men, Christopher said to himself, the appearance of good gave full cover to the evil. Nor was this surprising. The increase in man's power over Nature, in the nineteenth century and the early decades of the twentieth, appeared as an increase proportionate to man's stature in the scheme of things, a legitimate easing of the terms of his brief leasehold on earth ; and he called it Progress and thought that it was good.

But it was good only in so far as it was indeed proportionate. It is part of the splendour of the human body and the human mind that, in the endeavour to run, to swim, to climb, to break down obstacles in their path, to move, to discover and understand, to progress, they continually submit themselves to stress. The acceptance of this stress in its highest degrees is called valour, heroism, genius ; without it in some degree, existence is lifeless, mediocre and slothful. Yet if the claim to speed or power made by any limb of the body or any part of the mind is disproportionate to the capacity of the whole body or the whole mind, the result in the body is dislocation, in the mind *hubris*, in both unbalance and overthrow.

Nor, by an inexorable law, shall the whole body or the whole mind exceed the limits of its own nature. A man who, of his own strength unmechanized, attempts to jump a chasm of twenty-five feet may be an athlete and a hero, but if he attempt a hundred he is mad. . . . But are there inexorable limits to the mind of man ? Was he not made in God's image ? . . .

Even as he asked himself that question, Christopher recognized it as the question by which the intellect (as distinct from the intuition) of the contemporary world was being beguiled. Its subtlety and the difficulty of answering it and its temptation, he thought, lie in the fact that to God nothing is impossible. It follows logically that our limitations are not irremovable by him. In his timelessness, he is able to promote his creatures to omnipotence and omniscience. Nevertheless to dream of this is to dream madness. To presume it, and to guide our actions by the presumption, is blasphemy. The whole instinct of mankind has been opposed to this interpretation of the Immanent Will. The idea of limitation of our powers on earth has lain at the root of all religion, and the idea of ourselves as subject to time, to death, to external Nature, to the gods, at the root of all poetry. It is not from us that 'no secrets are hid'. Nor in our heart of hearts would we have it otherwise. Our genius is great, only in the proportion of our littleness. If we aspire to omnipotence, or even to such a degree of power as destroys that proportion, we forfeit the compassion and call down upon ourselves the anger and the ridicule of the gods. This is the accumulated wisdom of mankind, embodied in our legends — in the tale of Adam, of Icarus, of Faust, of Satan himself. And in the legend, Christopher thought, of Prometheus, who stole fire from heaven.

8

He became resolved, therefore, that he would withhold from men those very uses of the Burning Glass which would appear to enrich them — the civil, the industrial, the so-called 'beneficent' uses, which no government, no industry and no interpreter of the popular desire can now reject if they are made available. In this, he was not denying a natural hunger but an abnormal craving. He was refusing to lead mankind into temptation. For this is our power-predicament : that we have no means of collectively rejecting a distortion of our lives which intuitively we dread. We are addicts.

That men are conscious of the distortion of their lives is not yet self-evident ; the clamour for speed, for mechanized entertainment, for visits to the moon, would appear to deny it. And yet no sensitive mind can be unaware of a stirring of dread in the world — not only of fear that science is condemning civilization to bodily death, but of spiritual dread that life is being deprived of its order and proportion. Poets no longer sing of the brevity of life or of the sweetness and sadness of our condition ; they write, without singing, of its corruption and chaos, or of its longing for confession and absolution. In painting and sculpture, distortion is either admired as an expression of guilt or hated as a glorification of it : the guilt is recognized. Even the multitude of men whose counterparts, half a century ago, regarded life, however harsh it might be, as a recognizable sequence of cause and effect within the orbit of human frailty and free-will, have now a sense of the negation of all will, of the emptying out of meaning and purpose, of peace that is war, of a wild inconsequence in human affairs ; and yet of human power for ever increasing. The book of life was always hard to read because we were children who had not learned to decipher the handwriting, but we did not doubt in our hearts that it was readable. Now we are suddenly grown-up ; we are tall in power and rich in knowledge ; the book of life is neatly printed and lies open before us ; but the letters do not make words, the figures do not add up, the pictures are nightmares and the pages rise up against us like the walls of a prison.

To doubt that there is a way out is to acquiesce in chaos and to doubt God's mercy. History moves in phases ; the power-phase may be drawing to its close ; there may be a halt for many centuries in all but the minor developments of technology. There is reason to hope for this. Christopher Terriford is not the only man of science with the wisdom to desire it ; nor is it questionable that in the lay world, wherever thought is not frozen into a rigid pattern, men are beginning to outgrow the imagination of power as a self-vindicating end. But we need time in which to shake off the nightmare of the absence of God. Christopher Terriford's decision is no more than a refusal to plunge us deeper into it.

Of his decision to allow, nevertheless, the use of the Burning Glass in extreme military emergency against a totalitarian enemy, little more need be said than is said in the play itself. It is consistent with his resolve to give the world time to shake off the nightmare which totalitarianism would fasten upon it, for totalitarianism is a daemonic forbidding of the spirit of man to open its eyes.

CHARACTERS

(in order of appearance)

CHRISTOPHER TERRIFORD (34), *Head of the Terriford Research Unit*
MARY TERRIFORD (24), *his wife*
TONY LACK (perhaps 40), *his second at the Unit*
LADY TERRIFORD (59), *his mother*
TAMAS DOMOKOS (GERRY) HARDLIP (perhaps 38)
LORD HENRY STRAIT (35-45), *on the Prime Minister's personal staff*
MONTAGU WINTHROP (62 or more), *Prime Minister*
INSPECTOR WIGG, *a police officer*

SCENES

Place: The South Room at Terriford House, near Lamberton,
near the Channel, sixty miles from London

   Act I: A Monday evening before dinner in early September
   Act II: The same night, 1.30 A.M.
   Act III Scene 1: The following Sunday, near nightfall
                        2: Eight days later. Tea-time

Period: Soon

ACT I

ACT I

A room at Mitton, a large country-house sixty miles from London and near the Channel coast. The house was built in the middle of the eighteenth century and is to be thought of as being long and low. Half of it, known as the Private House, is still the home of CHRISTOPHER TERRI-FORD, *his young wife* MARY *and his mother* LADY TERRI-FORD; *the other half was converted in the nineteen-twenties by his father, Sir George Terriford, into a Meteorological Research Unit, particularly devoted to problems of Weather Control. Since his father's death, Christopher, who was his father's partner in research, has directed the Unit.*

This room in the Private House is large and beautiful, but friendly and very much lived-in. In the centre, upstage, is a wide bay shaped as the segment of a circle and raised by one step above the general floor level. A double door, partly of glass, occupies the middle of the bay's curving wall, and on each side of it is a window with a window-seat. The prospect is West of South so that, in the evening, sun-glow will flood in from the Left (the actors' Left). To the audience, nothing but sky is visible through the glass, for beyond the windows a great lawn falls away to the Lower Garden; but between the windows and the lawn is a secondary approach to Mitton through Mitton Woods, and when a car comes by this way (from Right to Left), intending to round the house's western end on its way to the front door on the north side, the sound of its engines may be heard.

On the Right (always actors' Right) of the bay, against the upper wall, is a grand piano, carrying a bronze bust, a lamp and flowers, and littered with music. This piano is set back into the up-Right corner of the room. A player faces Left. The upper wall on his left hand as he sits should contain a window if the set is large enough to allow both this and a window to balance it on the other side of the stage ; otherwise oil-paintings with picture lights.

In the centre of the Right Wall, below the piano, is a door which leads to other rooms in the Private House and ultimately to the staircase by which one goes to bed. It leads also to the Pass Door, at the foot of the staircase, by means of which the Private House communicates with the Unit. None of this is visible. The point is that whoever comes from the Unit, comes in Right.

Upstage in the Left Wall is another door which leads through an ante-room and hall to the front door. Again, none of this is visible. The point is that anyone who comes in from outside the house enters either through the bay (from the garden) or through the door Left.

Below the door Left is a fireplace with a leather-topped club-fender before it, and a large gilt-framed Regency looking-glass standing on the mantelpiece. Immediately above the fireplace and at right angles to it, a sofa runs out into the room. Near to the sofa or, perhaps, touching it is a formidable writing-table with a heavy ink-stand and at least one lamp. There are two telephones on this table : the black one connects with the exchange ; the white one, on which two numbers only are dialled, is a house-telephone connecting with other rooms in the Private House and with *the Unit. A third and green telephone will be added when the Prime Minister requires a secret line to Lamberton Manor.*

The other principal pieces of furniture are : a low chess-table, with an unfinished game set out on it, which stands in such a position near the fire that the two players could, if they wished, be seated, one on the sofa, the other on the upper end of the fender ; below the door Left, a bracket-clock, small and elegant, which chimes and strikes unobtrusively and rather merrily ; a low circular tea-table that can be moved without difficulty; at the writing-table, a high-backed writing-chair without arms, the occupant of which can turn rapidly while still seated ; at the end of the piano farther from the player (that is to say within easy reach of the bay), a small table on which drinks and glasses are always standing ; and, very important, downstage and Right of Centre, a single-ended sofa.

This sofa is a little in the Récamier manner but does not strictly follow that model. It is quilted and comfortable. Its scrolled end is high, so that, if you lie a little low, your head does not stand up above it. On the right of the scrolled end, the sofa has a low side-piece for about a third of its length so that, if you like, instead of lying on the sofa, you can sit comfortably in the corner, using the side-piece as a back.

The single-ended sofa is placed at an angle of about forty-five degrees to the footlights, its upper, scrolled end pointing at the door Right. Parallel with it, and at present on its downstage side, is a stool covered with papers and books — CHRISTOPHER'S *débris, for this sofa is particularly his. As he lies on it, he is able to see, in the mirror above the fireplace, a good deal of what is going on behind him. At the head of the sofa is a lamp on a pedestal.*

The general aspect of the room is much more that of a library than of a drawing-room. Large areas of the walls, where there happen not to be pictures, are covered to the ceiling with built-in book-shelves, and the room's appearance can be transformed by switching on shelf-lights as well as picture-lights, or any section of them. This may help the producer to give variety to a single set.

It is evening of early September about an hour before dinner. The curtains are back, for there is still daylight, but the lamp beside the single-ended sofa may be on, CHRISTOPHER *having been working there.*

He and his wife, MARY, *are discovered. He is a highly strung but self-controlled man of about thirty-five, with now and then a darting humour at his own expense and a tendency to be more surprised than impressed by his own intellect. He so values his private life that he dislikes intensely having 'importance' thrust upon him, but he is by no means a crank and, confronted with a power and responsibility that he did not seek, he makes his decisions firmly and un-hysterically and stands by them.* MARY *is of great value to him, partly because they deeply love each other (and this, in crisis, is sure ground under their feet), and partly because he is convinced that, though nearly ten years younger, she is intuitively wiser than he — and perhaps, spiritually, she is. She is beautiful and gentle, simple and direct ; so full of happiness and inward peace that nothing shakes her. The roots of her life are her love of God, which saves her from panic in the upheavals of the world ; her love of her husband, which gives her vitality and balance ; and her sense of*

6

proportion, which prevents her from condemning human frailty, even TONY LACK'S. *But because she is no respecter of persons, she has sometimes a certain ingenuous abruptness which the worldly wise have not, and when she finds herself opposed in conscience to the great and good (for example, to the Prime Minister), she says so in an unhesitating way that diplomatists would not recommend.*

At the moment she is standing, already dressed for dinner, at the head of the single-ended sofa. CHRISTOPHER *in day clothes is lying on it with his eyes shut, and she is taking away his headache by the movement of her hands on his forehead, a process which he enjoys. There is silence as the curtain rises. She stoops to kiss him gently on the forehead ; then, thinking he is asleep, lets her hands fall.*

CHRISTOPHER

Go on a little while.

MARY

I thought you were asleep.

CHRISTOPHER

I am, but not quite.

MARY

Is the headache gone ?

CHRISTOPHER

It might come back.

MARY

Then go to sleep. (*Using her hands again*) Go . . . to . . . sleep. You will need your strength to-night.

CHRISTOPHER

I wanted to forget that.

MARY

Forget it. Sleep, my darling, sleep.

CHRISTOPHER

And when each Jill has found her Jack
And three score sheep and nine have passed,
I'll clamber on the seventieth back
And ride to glory on the last.

And (*his voice dying away*) ride to . . . glory . . .
on the . . . (*Now he seems to be asleep. Through the door
Right, behind* MARY, TONY LACK *comes in. He is in full
evening dress — white tie and waistcoat — and extremely
elegant. He is older than* CHRISTOPHER *but nevertheless his
second-in-command at the Unit — a man of brilliant mind
but bruised character whose gaiety and rashness of manner,
spontaneous when he was younger, is now used as cover for
his sense of having been cheated by life. But whatever his
faults, lugubriousness is not among them ; he is a gallant
loser, always ready to play another hand. Towards women
he can't help being predatory, but he is not hard-hearted and
is fully capable of deep affection. His face lights up at finding, as he supposes, that* MARY *is alone, and he advances
with a smile and a lively step, beginning to say :*)

TONY

Mary, listen, before I go—— (*She commands silence
with a gesture. He tiptoes with exaggerated and mocking
caution, stands very close to her, looking over her shoulder.*)

8

TONY

'Peradventure he sleepeth?' (MARY *nods. As her hands are still on* CHRISTOPHER'S *forehead,* TONY *takes his opportunity to put his arm, caressingly and yet lightly enough to allow her not to take the gesture seriously, round her shoulders. It is only a touch, almost at once withdrawn. He is eager to make love to her but is keeping open a line of retreat.*) Then come and talk to me.

MARY

(*Who has, however, dropped her hands at his touch so that the physical link with her husband is momentarily lost*)
Please, Tony, not now. (*He hesitates an instant; then grasps that the circumstances are not propitious and retreats with grace. He picks up her hands and conveys them in the direction of* CHRISTOPHER'S *head.*)

TONY

Nice hands, but that (*ironically*) is where they belong. (*As he goes, she deliberately does not follow him with her eyes. When the door is shut and she has her hands on* CHRISTOPHER'S *forehead again, his hands come up and hold hers.*)

CHRISTOPHER

I'm glad you married me.

MARY

(*With a delighted smile*)
For a great man of science, you're a very bad patient. (*He raises himself and turns towards her.*) Don't leap about. You'll undo all the good. Lie down.

CHRISTOPHER

Then come down to me. (*He draws her down. She kneels on the floor beside him. She passionately kisses him and he holds her in his arms.*) That seems for the moment to solve all problems.

MARY

There aren't any.

CHRISTOPHER

Not even the Burning Glass ?

MARY

That isn't a problem between you and me ; only between us and the world.

CHRISTOPHER

This evening, unless Mother fails to land her Big Fish, the thing opens up, doesn't it ? How it opens up ! And how I hate it!

MARY

But you did agree in the end that the Prime Minister had to be asked.

CHRISTOPHER

Yes, I agreed in the end. (*Tenderly reproachful*) You didn't say anything against it.

MARY

I didn't say anything at all. Prime Ministers aren't the kind of thing I know about.

CHRISTOPHER

But, my sweetheart, you are practical enough, heaven knows.

MARY

Am I ? Not on that level. If I'm of any use to you, it's because I love you first for what you are ; only afterwards for what you do.

CHRISTOPHER

In a way, the Burning Glass does touch even that. Six weeks ago I was — well, just myself, and now I'm the kind of chap that Prime Ministers come to see. I feel almost a different being with that monstrous power over Nature in my hands — in *my* hands ! How much I tell the Prime Minister does go to the root of things. To be or not to be. Science has never yet kept back its knowledge. If it comes to that, mankind has never rejected power. We have always said : 'Ah, but this power has beneficent uses as well. Let's go for it !' We have never yet said : 'We are unfit for it.' The time may have come to say that.

MARY

It isn't a decision on the . . . on the Prime Minister level. That's what I meant. It isn't policy. It's like deciding whether to die for something or live for something. It is deep — inside *you*. Deeper than argument. One of those decisions that just can't be made when we argue ; only when we listen.

CHRISTOPHER

Or pray.

MARY

To pray is to listen, not to talk.

CHRISTOPHER

I have to decide to-night.

MARY

My darling, don't force it. You will decide naturally. When you are ready you will know what to do. (*This marks a period in their dialogue. She goes to the fireplace and from there says :*) Christopher, when you agreed that the Prime Minister should be invited, was that against your judgement?

CHRISTOPHER

He *had* to be. It *is* common sense. The Burning Glass had to go to that level as a matter of Defence. I saw it coming before this evening, and I have taken . . . certain steps provisionally. But it was against every private and personal wish I have. I'm not a man of power; I just don't deal in Prime Ministers. I have always thanked heaven I'm not an atomist and that this particular Terriford Unit has never been, in any military sense, on the secret list, in my father's time or in mine. Just Weather Control, if we could get it. Rain on parched land and . . . well, sunshine on Derby day, I suppose. It sounded beneficent and harmless, and I never wanted it otherwise.

MARY

Tony doesn't see it in that way.

CHRISTOPHER

Oh, I know. More than half of him has always wished our job weren't so damned civilian. Some people are

. . . so made. The very words Top Secret give them a thrill. Tony's like that. So is his curious friend Gerry Hardlip. From their point of view, I'm a babe unborn.

MARY

That is why I love you.

CHRISTOPHER

Because I'm a babe unborn?

MARY

Because from their point of view you are. . . . Oh, I'm bad about Mr. Hardlip. I feel about him as I should be ashamed to feel about a snake.

CHRISTOPHER

I confess it surprises me that Tony finds him companionable. . . . Why was Tony all dressed up — white tie, white waistcoat?

MARY

You were supposed to be asleep.

CHRISTOPHER

Doors click. Eyes open. There's a perfectly good mirror over there.

MARY

So there is.

CHRISTOPHER
(*After a pause*)

Mary, how tiresome is he?

MARY

Tony? To me? Not at all. Why he wants to flirt with me I don't know — he who can have twenty women.

CHRISTOPHER

And does — or did. . . . He isn't . . . so tiresome
. . . that you want him to go ?

MARY

From this house ? From the Unit ?

CHRISTOPHER

Either or both if you wish it.

MARY

There's no need. He's your friend . . . and mine,
Christopher. Only eighteen months ago he was our best
man. As your scientific partner, he's valuable, isn't he ?

CHRISTOPHER

Enormously.

MARY

(*As though that settled it*)

Well, then . . .

CHRISTOPHER

You said 'flirt with me'. He's going through a kind
of hell, I believe. I only thought that 'flirt' was too . . .
gentle a word ?

MARY

Not if you see the thing in my way.

CHRISTOPHER

He doesn't.

MARY

But I do.

14

CHRISTOPHER

(*Smiling at her calm, unshakable absolutism*)
I was only trying to rescue you, my sweetheart.

MARY

You did that eighteen months ago once and for all.
. . . Tony isn't what troubles me.

CHRISTOPHER
What does?

MARY

(*She sighs. They have talked about it so often
during the last six weeks*)
The Burning Glass. We always come back to it.

CHRISTOPHER
You said that wasn't a problem between you and me.

MARY

That is true. But it affects us. Since you made that
discovery six weeks ago, we have become — jointly, I
mean — quite different in . . . in our relationship to
other people. We didn't have any power over them;
they had none over us. There was nothing we deeply
valued that the world could give or take away —
certainly not our peace of mind. Now . . .

CHRISTOPHER
My dearest, isn't that still true?

MARY

Not quite.

CHRISTOPHER

What has it taken from us?

MARY

The simplicities. The blessed fact that from — well from Tony's point of view or from the Prime Minister's if it comes to that — we were as unimportant as a bank clerk . . . or a poet. Our walks, our special trees, the books we shared and the music, the tricks we used to play with your miraculous memory — and mine, our games of blindfold chess when your day's work was over . . . (*She is trying to express something intensely personal that she can't quite express, and so she is not finishing her sentences.*) Our *little* things . . . they were our life . . . and the Burning Glass has changed their proportion. Look——

CHRISTOPHER

At what?

MARY

Our chess-table. (*They are beside it.*) We were playing that game . . . so long ago that it wants dusting. (*She lifts up a piece and takes his handkerchief with which to dust it.*)

CHRISTOPHER

We'll finish it to-night.

MARY

In spite of the Prime Minister? (*She puts the piece back.*)

CHRISTOPHER

When he's gone.

MARY

When he's gone !

CHRISTOPHER

(*Taking her in his arms*)

My dearest, I know what you mean. This thing breaks in.

MARY

Now, when we are . . . lovers, even that isn't any longer just our two selves. It has become also a shutting out of 'this thing'. Our private peace was something we didn't know we had to defend. Now we have to.

CHRISTOPHER

(*Almost throwing the words away because there is nothing between them that is not instantly understood*)

From all the crafts and assaults of the devil.

MARY

Your mother would say that was medieval.

CHRISTOPHER

My dear mother ? I wonder sometimes. She's such a queer mixture of polite convention and of *feeling* for herself — and, half the time, covering even that with small talk. If you're ill, send for the doctor ; if there's a fire, send for the fire-brigade ; if you find out how to harness the sun, send for the Prime Minister. To her, knowledge is always Progress. It always was among the men of science of my father's day. No devils for them. . . . Mary, before she comes, there's something I want you to do. You have a memory.

MARY

Not yours, but yes — visually very strong.

CHRISTOPHER

For example that chess-board. Keep your back to it. You looked at it just now.

MARY

I wasn't trying to remember it.

CHRISTOPHER

No, but you examined it. Could you now give me the positions?

MARY

Of course. White: base-line: two blanks; Rook, Queen, blank, Rook, King, blank. Second line: two blanks; Bishop, two Knights, two Pawns, blank.[1] Third line——

CHRISTOPHER
(*Laughing*)

Good. Bless you. But the day after to-morrow? Would it still be there?

MARY

Possibly not. I wasn't trying to plant the memory. It isn't planted deep.

CHRISTOPHER

If you had been trying, it would be?

[1] Lasker *v.* Blackburne, 1899 (Tartakower and du Mont, *500 Master Games of Chess*, p. 67).

MARY

What am I to remember?

CHRISTOPHER

(*Giving her a piece of paper*)

This.

MARY

What is it?

CHRISTOPHER

It is the Upper Intensity Setting on Machine Six —
the one which produces the effect of the Burning Glass.

MARY

The Upper Setting? Are there two?

CHRISTOPHER

Upper and Lower. That (*the paper*) is a half — less
than a half, strictly — of what I carry in my own mind.

MARY

I don't understand.

CHRISTOPHER

For a moment, don't try to. I will explain. Read it.
Eleven five-figure groups and three non-active zeros.
Photograph it in your mind. This time, plant it deep.
(*She gazes at it and, from time to time, after his mother is
come,* MARY *will gaze at it again.*)

MARY

If it is in writing, here, on this paper, why must I
memorize it?

CHRISTOPHER

Because it won't stay in writing. Not for anyone. Not for the Prime Minister. If anything should happen to me, I want a half of the setting to exist in your memory alone. It gives you an absolute veto on the use of the Burning Glass. One part is there, in your hands. The other I have sent—— (LADY TERRIFORD *enters. She was evidently a pretty girl forty years ago. Her gentle common sense has an overlay of Edwardian incisiveness. She is a woman of the world but by no means a worldly woman.*)

LADY TERRIFORD

Well, it's done.

CHRISTOPHER
(*To* MARY)

Plant it deep.

LADY TERRIFORD

Who would have believed that Monty Winthrop — who was really an exceedingly quick and intuitive young man when we danced together — could become so dense as Prime Minister. . . . But perhaps it isn't his fault. Telephones are really a great handicap to women.

CHRISTOPHER

Few appear to think so.

LADY TERRIFORD

Well, my dear, it's all a question of how you were brought up. A smile is a weapon or should be. So is an eyebrow. So is a letter if tactfully written — so much can be conveyed by starting a new sentence and not

20

quite crossing out the old one. But of course if a woman is illiterate or has no eyebrows, she takes to the telephone, quack, quack, like a duck to a puddle.

MARY

You persuaded Mr. Winthrop, all the same?

LADY TERRIFORD

But I had to play a lot of trumps. I dislike that. When I got through to the Manor, I didn't ask for his host, but for the Prime Minister himself. A young man on his staff spoke to me first. Very young, very courteous, very pink and clean; even on the telephone one almost smelt the soap. He was soothing and plummy, like the B.B.C. announcing the death of a film star to an audience of twelve million half-wits.

CHRISTOPHER

There may not be twelve million half-wits.

LADY TERRIFORD

That is what the B.B.C. appear so often to forget. . . .

CHRISTOPHER

What happened then?

LADY TERRIFORD

Then Lord Henry Strait came to the abominable instrument. (*To* MARY, *whose eyes are on her paper:*) My dear, what are you studying so intently? The cross-word?

21

MARY

(*Who has been planting it deep*)

No.

LADY TERRIFORD

Because I have done it. 'Conflagration, in the White House, perhaps' is, quite obviously, Casabianca. How I hate the word 'perhaps'. It always means the man is cheating. Or do you think that crosswords are composed by women?

CHRISTOPHER

(*Angrily*)

What did Lord Henry say? . . . Mother why are you prattling? Of all times now? I hate clever-clever Edwardian prattle as much as the cling-clang of a modern cocktail party. And it's not in your nature. (*He has spoken so sharply — and it is a mark of the tension in him that he is impatient with the mother he respects and loves — that* MARY *comes up to take his arm and steady him.*)

MARY

Gentle.

CHRISTOPHER

(*Not gently*)

I am gentle. But why now? (*But he goes over to his mother and, still trembling, puts his hand on her shoulder, and says — gently:*) Why now, Mamma?

LADY TERRIFORD

Only because I am tired, my dearest. When a thing is too serious to be . . . easily borne, it is often best to

talk nonsense for a little while. At least so I was taught.
. . . Some people, when the world looks ugly, are
silent ; I prattle in its ugly face. You must allow to each
generation its own idiom. . . . In any case the Prime
Minister is coming.

CHRISTOPHER

At what time ?

LADY TERRIFORD

Not to dinner. Late. They have a large dinner-party.
He and Lord Henry were to have left by car at eleven-
fifteen and to have been in Downing Street before one.
I said : 'Two will do. You can spend an hour here.'
But he was stubborn. He had to know why. And when
I said, 'Because I ask it,' that little trump wasn't big
enough to take the trick. He said, 'Yes, my dear Helen,
for forty years that has been the best of reasons, but
still—' (*She sighs — at her own expense.*) But still !
But still ! . . . One's little trumps grow smaller with the
years. . . . (*And she drifts into the silence of her private
recollection.*)

CHRISTOPHER

And so you played the ace ?

LADY TERRIFORD

Strictly, my dear, the Queen. I knew, with him, she
headed all the suits. I told him that the national interest
required him to come. And I had to add —how I
detest it ! — that what I had to say could not be said
on an open telephone.

CHRISTOPHER

I suppose that is true.

LADY TERRIFORD

It is horrible that it should be true ! It isn't a pretty world in which, on a September evening within sixty miles of London, you daren't speak openly on your own telephone.

MARY

(*Who, since she last spoke has been listening intently, the paper loose and visible in her hand*)

It isn't a pretty world . . . outwardly. But it ought to be simple in one's own conscience. And it's not.

LADY TERRIFORD

Conscience is a great book but a difficult one. I used to think it was an easy text-book on conduct that would tell me exactly what to do ; but it isn't, you know. It is a great work of art, and we, who are children, have to learn to read it — not without tears. Forgive me if I say that I think you and Christopher are learning to read it too (*and she makes a joke of the word*) compli-cate-edly.

MARY

(*It is not a question*)

Or too simply.

LADY TERRIFORD

Perhaps we mean the same thing. (*To her son*) You know, Christopher, if what has happened to you had happened to your father — I mean, if his science had put into his hands this overwhelming power, it would never have entered his mind to keep that knowledge to himself and let it die with him. And, after all, your own impulse was the same. In the first place, you didn't keep it to yourself.

CHRISTOPHER
(*And he speaks less to her than to himself, with a quickening tempo of self-discovery*)

Because at that time, when the Reflex Indicators, quite suddenly, gave me that *effect*, I didn't see it as a military effect. I didn't see it even as an industrial effect — an infinite supply of pure heat, spilling out from heaven just because my puny hand turns on the tap. . . . Or spilling out of hell . . . I didn't then see it in that way at all, but as a scientific result. It was much as if I had been playing the piano and a miracle had happened, and such music had come out of it as 'never was on sea or land'. . . . I leapt up from Machine Six. I switched off the power and left the setting. I came running out——

LADY TERRIFORD
And told *me*——

CHRISTOPHER
(*And now he has come back, humorously to little things*)
Didn't I always tell you when I won a prize at school?

LADY TERRIFORD
And Mary? And Mr. Tony Lack?

25

CHRISTOPHER

Well, he's my partner in Weather Control. If, quite suddenly, you get the hell of a result, isn't it natural to say, 'Tony, come and look! Come and look at this!'

LADY TERRIFORD

You took him to Machine Six and he saw the setting?

CHRISTOPHER

We switched on. He saw the result in the Indicators and he saw the setting and I broke the setting up.

LADY TERRIFORD

But it is in your mind?

CHRISTOPHER

Of course.

LADY TERRIFORD

Then why not in his?

CHRISTOPHER

Because, because, because . . . he hasn't that freak of memory. He couldn't remember the positions of a chess-board, much less——

LADY TERRIFORD

One minute. I want to get this clear. I know and Mary knows and Mr. Tony Lack knows that the Burning Glass exists, but, except you, no one knows how to . . . to apply it?

CHRISTOPHER

No one.

LADY TERRIFORD

Not Mr. Tony?

CHRISTOPHER

No one.

LADY TERRIFORD

Doesn't it trouble him that you haven't given him the . . . setting? (CHRISTOPHER *does not answer*.) He is your partner in Weather Control. This is, or was, part of it. You give him the result, but not the means. Has he asked for the setting? (CHRISTOPHER *is silent, not wishing to answer*.)

MARY

Has he, Christopher?

CHRISTOPHER

Yes.

MARY

More than once?

CHRISTOPHER

Twice, in a casual way. As you know I have experimented since. . . . Mother, what are you getting at? I don't distrust him, but this thing is new; I want time to get the dimensions of it. Certainly, as you say, Tony is my partner in Weather Control. But the Burning Glass is as different from that as a jet bomber from a kite. It gives us power, by use of the sun's rays, to burn up the earth or any part of it. As I see it, that opens a new volume in your book of conscience. Almost a new language. And I'm trying to learn to read it; Mary knows. So meanwhile I have shut up. I haven't given Tony the know-how, or Mary, or you.

LADY TERRIFORD

You see, my dear, Mr. Tony has, in my judgement (*and she chooses the word*), adhesive friends. There is, for example, this Mr. Hardlip who comes now and then. Is his name Hardlip?

CHRISTOPHER

It is an adaptation of his name to make it pronounceable. . . . You mustn't be prejudiced, Mamma, although I know you like to call a spade a spade.

LADY TERRIFORD

That isn't the point. I like a spade to call *itself* a spade. (CHRISTOPHER *makes a gesture of despair at her suspicions and says to* MARY:)

CHRISTOPHER

Why was Tony all dressed up? You didn't tell me that.

MARY

A party.

CHRISTOPHER

In London?

MARY

Mr. Hardlip is calling and driving him up.

CHRISTOPHER

That is impossible now. If the Prime Minister is coming Tony must be here. (*He goes to the house-telephone and dials two numbers.*) No answer from his bedroom. I take it, he has gone across to the Unit to fortify himself. (*Dials again.*) Unit? . . . Terriford. . . . Mr. Lack there? . . . No, I don't want him on the telephone. . . . Ask him, from me, to come over to the Private House when he's finished his drink. . . . Not urgent, but important — when he's finished his drink. . . . Understood? . . . (*To Mary*) You are dressed! I must at least put on a black tie. And you, too, Mamma. (LADY TERRIFORD *rises. She and he move towards door Right. Then he turns back to his wife.*) Is that (*he takes the paper from her*) firm in your mind?

MARY

Yes.

CHRISTOPHER

Planted deep?

MARY

I shan't forget it.

CHRISTOPHER

Then I can burn this. (*While he does so, she says:*)

MARY

What am I to do with it?

CHRISTOPHER

I'll tell you later.

29

LADY TERRIFORD

What is it?

CHRISTOPHER

One of our memory games. . . . When Tony comes, Mary, tell him from me he must wash out his party for to-night.

MARY

He will say no.

CHRISTOPHER

With the Prime Minister coming?

MARY

All the more. The great and good always make him shrug his rebellious shoulders.

CHRISTOPHER

Not on his job. It is his job to be here. Tell him.

MARY

If you say so.

CHRISTOPHER

Mamma, when you were talking to the Prime Minister, why did you insist that he should come to-night?

LADY TERRIFORD
(*Guardedly*)

He happens to be at the Manor, ten minutes away.

CHRISTOPHER

Is so small a convenience worth so many trumps?

LADY TERRIFORD
No, if you put it so.

CHRISTOPHER
I could have gone to him. It might have been politer, heaven knows. Why here, to-night, at all costs?

LADY TERRIFORD
Intuition. . . . I am sorry, my dear, I am a common-sensical person and intuition, I dare say, isn't in my part. . . . But I am not comfortable this evening. There are some days in life that one would like to be safely over. No doubt, I shall be more intelligent after a hot bath. (*She goes out Right.* CHRISTOPHER *looks at the chess-table with longing and reaches for* MARY'S *hand.*)

CHRISTOPHER
After he's gone, we'll finish that game.

MARY
That particular game? . . . Or chess?

CHRISTOPHER
That particular. We began it so long ago. Con-tinuity. Private life. Peaceful life. I don't know. . . . But I do know I want to finish that game before we sleep.

MARY
Good. You are a funny one, my darling. Don't make too big a symbol of too small a thing. Suppose someone upset the table?

CHRISTOPHER

(*In real alarm*)

Why do you say that? Why do you say that? (*Then with relief*) Even if someone did, you'd remember the positions. You would put it together again. . . . Now, forward into battle. (*As he crosses Right*, TONY LACK *enters through the door which* LADY TERRIFORD *left open.*)

TONY

(*Smiling*)

What has happened? I came in from the Unit through the pass door. There was your mother beginning to negotiate the stairs. She looked at me as if I were the ghost of Hamlet's father. I said — I oughtn't to have, of course.

MARY

What did you say?

TONY

I said: 'Angels and ministers of grace, defend us.' And she said: 'Yes, indeed.' What does one make of that?

CHRISTOPHER

Are you going to London to-night?

TONY

Yes, indeed.

CHRISTOPHER

You can't.

TONY

Can't I?

CHRISTOPHER

Mary will tell you why. (*He goes.*)

TONY

What is all this?

MARY

(*Soothing his evident excitement*)

Sit down peacefully.

TONY

(*Not obeying*)

You are quite right. I have, as you perceive, had three doubles. But I can take that.

MARY

(*Cheerfully playing with and not against his mood*)

If you will, out of consideration for us, not dine out in London to-night, and take off your white tie——

TONY

As for the tie, that's easy. (*He rips it off.*) Always your obedient servant.

MARY

(*And she can't help smiling at that*)

Not always obedient.

TONY

I was born masterful where beautiful women are concerned — a Casanova of the cradle, a Byron of the bassinet. (*From this moment onward the scene between them is, so to speak, an exercise in counterpoint. His rash and insensate love-making (insensate because without*

33

hope) clashes with his fear that he may have already said too much to Hardlip, and both these clash with her gentleness, her self-control, her determination to hold firmly to the theme of the Prime Minister's coming. The speed is to be very high in bursts, with intervening slow passages; the volume of sound is to be marked by violent contrasts like a night-sea on a beach.)

MARY

The Prime Minister has been staying at the Manor. He is coming here after dinner on his way back to London. Christopher wants you to stay. (*Rather late:*) So do I.

TONY

I shall do nothing of the kind. Prime Ministers as a species are not my cup of tea. Nor do I want tea. In any case, why is he coming?

MARY

Be serious, Tony.

TONY

I was trying, out of consideration for you, not to be. The only thing I want to be serious about is you, which doesn't please you, I can't think why.

MARY

Yes you can.

TONY

Oh, you are married and love your husband and so on, I know that; I don't really blame you for saying no, but why should you blame me for asking? You can regard it, if you please, as a politeness. It's so much

34

pleasanter for a woman to say no, than never to be asked at all. Be honest, isn't it? Unless the chap bores you. And I don't . . . Or do I?

MARY

No.

TONY

Well, then, I revert to the previous question. . . . Isn't it?

MARY

(*Smiling*)

Not if one's happy, Tony . . . and if one doesn't want to make the other chap unhappy and——

TONY

And drink three doubles? Now, whatever else you are, you aren't the guardian angel of my wine-bill. In fact, I am so made that I link women with song, not with wine. That is why I'm going on a stag-party to-night, *faute de mieux*. (*Prestissimo*) The Porter in Macbeth, you know, said a mouthful on the subject of wine and women. 'Lechery it provokes and unprovokes. It makes him stand to and not stand to. It droppeth as the gentle rain from heaven. 'Tis mightiest in the mightiest. It becomes the thronèd monarch better than his crown.' (MARY *breaks out laughing*.) Or has Scotland wandered into Venice? I *must* learn not to telescope the plays of Shakespeare! It leads one into every kind of moral entanglement. . . . (*Rallentando*) Very well, I revert from poetry to prose. Why do you steadfastly refuse to discuss the one subject I want to talk about?

MARY

I don't, if you would talk sense.

TONY

You want to talk about Prime Ministers. (*Allegro*)
It is, I grant you, a solemn subject, a noble subject, a
pompous-historical subject, but it is not a sensual one.
(*There is a silence, during which* MARY *makes a long move —
away and back again. They have been fencing. Now the
tone hardens.*)

MARY

Tony, I'm not a fool. Lately, you have seemed almost
to hate Christopher — and, sometimes, me. I know
quite well that, though you . . . prattle . . . as if it
were, this isn't a . . . a flirtation. (*Swiftly and with
intent*) And I know your value. And I know you are
going through some kind of hell. And I want — for my
own sake, not only for yours — I want not to be a blind,
selfish fool.

TONY

And so ?

MARY

How can I be of any use ? What, in reason, do you
want ?

TONY

To go to bed with you. . . . Well, I'm not sorry.
You asked me. I thought you played chess. Princess's
opening accepted. Knight's gambit declined. Why are
there no princesses in that lamentable game ?

MARY

Since you are direct, so will I be. Why do you want to go to bed with me?

TONY

Pleasure. You would be charming naked. And one would forget the twentieth century, and the Burning Glass would make no odds. . . . Isn't that a good reason?

MARY

But not the whole reason? There are other women as good . . . naked. Why do you want *me*?

TONY

Because, when I thought I was through with all that, you have cropped up as the one . . . sentimentality in my life that I haven't annihilated. I want to press that grape and spit out the skin. And that would be that.

MARY

'Sentimentality.'

TONY

Remove the quotes and call it love. You see, you believe in . . . you represent . . . you *are* all the things in which I used to believe. Including loyalty. Oh yes, I know. . . .

MARY

And so you wish to destroy them.

TONY

Since I can't regain them. Milton knew what he was talking about. Trust a Puritan to know the Devil. As

it is . . . put a bracket round one night . . . or two.
Wouldn't it be pleasurable? Be honest, wouldn't it?
Even the young and beautiful grow old.

MARY

No.

TONY

Are you saying it wouldn't be pleasurable or are you
just saying No?

MARY

I am saying No.

TONY

And then one is buried, and no one cares a damn.

MARY

What were the things, in which you once believed,
that I now represent? (*At that* TONY, *with an outfling
of his arms, walks right away from her and says:*)

TONY

Ah, if you take that ground . . . Angels and ministers
of grace defend you. That's the trouble — they do.
That is why I love you. (*Then he turns back.*) All right.
You win.

MARY

And now, please, will you give me a real answer
about the other thing?

TONY

What do you want to know?

MARY

Will you, when this Mr. . . . Hardlip comes, send him about his business ?

TONY

No. I should despise myself if I did.

MARY

Is your evening with him so important ?

TONY

Not in the least. That is why I go. You miss the point. In any genuine view of the world — yours, the Christian, or mine, the nihilistic view — the Prime Minister isn't important either. In certain moods we pretend he is ; we were brought up that way, it is our convention ; but he isn't. Christopher thinks I'm interested in power, and in a sense it's true. I can't altogether resist the trappings, again because I happen to have been brought up that way. If I had a chance, no doubt I'd be with joy Her Majesty's Principal Secretary of State for Foreign Affairs, or the First Sea Lord my luckless father might have been, or, best of all, Lord Bishop of Bath and Wells ; nothing so magnificently combines cleanliness with godliness as a Bishop of Bath and Wells. I should jump at any of those jobs with delight but only with the same delight I should have in being the Black Prince on a rocking-horse. Only to laugh at my silly self in fancy dress.

MARY

And so you are not what Mr. Hardlip is ?

TONY

What is 'Mr. Hardlip' ?

MARY

Tony, how much do you really know of him ? Where was he born ?

TONY

Vaguely on the Danube. A very cosmopolitan river, I grant you, not now as blue as it was.

MARY

And where brought up ?

TONY

Vaguely Brooklyn. Since then he has taken all the scholarships.

MARY

I'm sure he has. What happened during the war ?

TONY

The Economic Section of the Ministry of This and That. No fault of his. One of his hands doesn't function. He writes with his left. I suppose he's one of the very star economists at either University. I find him astringent at a party — like the vinegar in a salad dressing. Why all this interest in Gerry Hardlip ?

MARY

He's so different from you.

40

TONY

Ah, he takes himself seriously. He hates what he calls the System.

MARY

Ours ? The British ? The West ?

TONY

Much more than that : freedom, love, faith — all the romantic superstitions.

MARY

But, Tony, you too have renounced them.

TONY

Have I ? They have renounced me. My nursery is shut, that's all ; he never had one. I am *déraciné*. He is *by nature* an intellectual cosh-boy.

MARY

But you spend time with him.

TONY

(*Ruefully*)

I can't help it.

MARY

Why ?

TONY

I can't help it.

MARY

Why ?

TONY

A drug.

41

MARY

Against what?

TONY

Myself, you fool. You complacent, Christian fool.
. . . (*He sweeps her into his arms.*) Myself, you —
beloved, blind, wise adored one, whom I strip with my
eyes and my hands and my cruelty, and worship on my
knees and with my head, and hate with all the envies of
my soul. (*And now he breaks away and sits, not looking
at her, examining his own outstretched hands as though he
expected to find blood upon them.*) You say nothing.
(*She comes close to him and stands silently.*) Thou foster-
child of silence and slow time! (*She takes his hand and
holds it to reassure and steady him. He formally kisses her
hand and releases it.*) A great lady never makes a scene.
. . . I am glad the Prime Minister is coming.

MARY

(*Who has been left behind by this sudden change*)
What did you say?

TONY

I am glad the Prime Minister is to be told.

MARY

But you will take no part in it?

TONY

No.

MARY

Then how does it affect you? Why are you glad?

THE BURNING GLASS

TONY

(*He had been going to say much more but now
slides away from it*)

Oh . . . it puts the thing on the right footing.

MARY

What is it you are trying — *not* to say ?

TONY

Nothing. . . . Listen, Mary, what you said just now
— about my seeming to hate Christopher sometimes, it
isn't true. (*The nervous and passionate intensity of the
denial is, perhaps, an admission of the half-truth.*) I'm
not Iago, believe me. Whatever I may have said — or
done (*it is the 'saying' which is tormenting his mind and
the word 'done' is added hastily as an afterthought or
'cover'*) — hasn't been said or done in hatred of him. Or
even jealousy. My little madness is self-contained. I
want *you* : not to take you from *him*. I don't love you
in relation to your circumstances — least of all your
husband — but ringed round, isolatedly, Miranda on her
island. My island of which I've lost the chart. As far
as possible removed from Gerry Hardlip's stud-farm for
the communal intelligentsia. *A la recherche de l'âme
perdu !* . . . What am I talking about ?

MARY

You were telling me why you are glad that the Prime
Minister is coming to-night.

TONY

Because it will make Christopher safe — as safe as it
is humanly possible for him to be ever again.

43

MARY

Why, is he in . . . that kind of danger? Only we know even that the power exists.

TONY

(*Airily; he is avoiding the real answer*)

One can never be sure. Believe me, the rumour of such things gets into the air. Great power smells and the smell goes round the world — not the detail, but the smell.

MARY

How can it, if no one talks?

TONY

It can. Long before Hiroshima, it was known that that power existed. However you try to divide science into water-tight compartments, the compartments leak. (*He is becoming excited.*) It isn't necessary for you or me to go out and sell the Burning Glass setting to an enemy agent for a ruby necklace and a ton of caviare. Besides, we haven't got it to sell. All the same, when men all over the world, working on parallel lines, are waiting for the scientific cat to make its next jump, one word, the tone of a voice, an air of excitement, the *refusal* of an answer, is enough to make them say——

MARY

Say what?

TONY

(*He has been talking fast and loud. Now he drops his voice*)

Might be enough to make them say : 'My God, in the

44

Terriford Unit a very big cat *has* jumped' and might lead them to . . . You see what I mean ?

MARY

You are frightened, Tony. Is that why you stood out against Christopher's going to the Vienna Congress ?

TONY

Yes.

MARY

At first you wanted him to. You suggested it. And then you were fierce against it. Why, if you weren't frightened before ?

TONY

Because — (*He goes and mixes himself a drink while she waits.*) Because while I was shaving one morning, I remembered it was Gerry Hardlip who put the idea of the Vienna Meteorological Congress into my mind. And it wasn't *me* he wanted to go.

MARY

You thought Christopher wouldn't come back.

TONY

I thought he might not.

MARY

If there was danger of that kind, they could take him any afternoon when he goes out walking in Mitton Woods.

TONY

At the moment they prefer a cold war to a hot. Wouldn't it be more convenient to them if he voluntarily didn't come home from Vienna ? . . . Are you sure the Prime Minister is coming to-night ?

MARY

Quite sure.

TONY

Then from to-morrow all is well. There'll be a cordon round this house. No more solitary walks in Mitton Woods. No more vague honeymoons for you, my dear, wandering in Italian hill-towns. You will have a guard under your window and another at your bedroom door. (*A car sweeps up outside the french windows and stops.*)

TONY

Hardlip's car.

HARDLIP
(*Off*)

Are you ready ? Can I come in ?

MARY

Don't let him in here. Make him go round to the door.

TONY
(*At the window, waves the car on*)

Go on ! Go round to the door. We're barred and bolted here. I'll let you in. (*To* MARY) Wait and receive him.

MARY

No.

TONY

He must have seen you here.

MARY

Tony. (*He turns as he is going out of the door Left.*)
Don't mention the Prime Minister.

TONY

Cut out my tongue. (*He goes. She stands listening
to the bang of an outer door and the sound of the men's
voices as they come across the hall.*)

TONY

(*Off*)

Where are we to dine?

HARDLIP

(*Off*)

The Fourteen Club. The others meet us there. We
pick up this girl of Sellin's on the way. (MARY *goes. Her
going is just visible to them as they enter.*)

TONY

Then we ought to start.

HARDLIP

Time enough. She lives on the way to London. I
have left Sellin in the car. He can wait.

47

TONY

Bring the poor devil in. (*At the drink table.*) What do you want?

HARDLIP

Nothing. . . . No. He can wait. He wouldn't be approved of in this house. (*He has sat but rises again. He can't be still, but is perpetually fidgeting and fingering something.*) Nor, quite obviously, am I.

TONY

She had to dress.

HARDLIP

She was dressed.

TONY

She may have wished to change her dress.

HARDLIP

Do women dress twice for dinner?

TONY

Lord Almighty, why not if it amuses them?

HARDLIP

You needn't bother to cover her tracks. You know as well as I do that if the most boring curate had appeared at this moment, she'd have stayed and done her stuff, wouldn't she? And given him a glass of sherry, and asked after his grubby ecclesiastical spawn? At sight of me, she goes.

TONY

Do you mind?

48

HARDLIP

What she thinks of me? Not in the least! But you do. . . . Oh, I admit that, when you're with me or drunk, you have moments of emancipation. But an Englishman, when sober, is a domestic animal. Even when he conquers an empire, he takes out his own women and their afternoon tea. He would have been cosy with Cleopatra. In bed or battle, his highest reward is to be called a good boy. What you really want of Mary Terriford is not to possess her but that she shall love you and respect you, and kiss you on the forehead and tuck you up in bed. . . . 'Please, Nannie, may I go out to a party with Gerry to-night?' . . . 'Oh, Tony, do you think you ought to go out with naughty little backroom boys?' Isn't that what you were saying when I came in?

TONY

My God, what do you and I get out of each other's company?

HARDLIP

A masochistic pleasure. We enjoy the jab of each other's knives. . . . Anyhow, what was the result? Was milord Byron defiant? Or did Tony yield to persuasion, little by little? In either case, the rule stands. All the English are really in love with their nurses. That is why they make love so badly . . . (*a meditative afterthought*) and why, I suppose, they always win the last battle : they fight it with their backs to the nursery wall.

49

TONY

And why they get under your skin?

HARDLIP

On the contrary. I value them enormously. They provide a background to my intelligence. They admit me to their colleges because they need my brains, and to their clubs — some clubs — because they need my subscriptions. Their talent is to absorb; to receive external stimulus. Hence the Normans. Hence Disraeli. Hence myself. The English have always admitted foreigners, because their own company is so intolerably boring. But the accent remains on the word ' admit '.

TONY

Even among those you so innocently call ' the smart '?

HARDLIP

Ah, they are different! So are the proletariat. They have achieved the nihilism of the night-clubs and the gutter. They are the realists of the world to come. I love the proletariat because they have no mercy. I love the smart because they have no loyalties. I——

TONY

I love camellias because they have no smell! . . . Come off it, Gerry. I can't have you making a philosophy of your appetites.

HARDLIP

It is a habit among moral reformers. Besides, my appetites are under strict control.

TONY

Then your reputation flatters you. I gathered that
the smart admit you not infrequently to their beds.

HARDLIP

Poor darlings. The British are more bored in bed
than anywhere in the world. They welcome a moment
of educative depravity.

TONY

Then I don't see what you have to complain of.

HARDLIP

For myself, nothing. There is no country into
which it is more profitable to be naturalized. I am
extremely well paid for taking everything I want, and
I remain completely independent. But you don't.
You have the capacity to go to the very top — and
look at you : Terriford's assistant, dangling at the
apron-strings of Terriford's wife, holding the wool for
Terriford's mother ! . . . Those two women ! Different generations. Different ideas. But on one point
absolutely united and unswerving. They loathe my
guts. They keep me out and they keep you in. (TONY's
hand is on the decanter.) You won't need that drink
if you are coming to my party.

TONY

Listen, Gerry. How much difference would it
make if I didn't ?

HARDLIP

Please yourself. By all means stay, if you want full marks from teacher.

TONY

The point is this——

HARDLIP

Don't trouble to make excuses. Far be it from me to come between a man and his nurse.

TONY

There's no question of that. Mary has nothing whatever to do with it. It's a question of work.

HARDLIP

To-night?

TONY

Yes.

HARDLIP

In full evening-dress? . . . Tell me, why is your white tie hanging round your neck?

TONY

(*His hands go up. He is intensely embarrassed*) I can't imagine! (*He ties it.*)

HARDLIP

It looks like apron-strings. . . . You're a bad liar, Tony.

TONY

I tell you, this isn't personal to me or to you or to her. It is work. There is to be — well, if you want to know, some pretty important high-ups are coming in for a conference after dinner.

HARDLIP

(*Not a question*)

On the subject you told me of at Cambridge.

TONY

(*Airily*)

Among other things.

HARDLIP

I thought Christopher Terriford had some quixotic notion of keeping that discovery to himself and letting it die with him.

TONY

Did I say that?

HARDLIP

Don't you remember what you said? . . . More than you ought, Tony.

TONY

What did I tell you?

HARDLIP

For example, that the power exists and the nature of it.

53

TONY

(*Frightened, and trying to reassure himself*)

What does that matter? I never gave you the setting. Whatever I may have said that evening, I didn't give you that. I can't have, because I don't know it. I don't know it. (*Both are standing.*)

HARDLIP

Thank you. Your hysteria convinces me.

TONY

Of what?

HARDLIP

That you really don't know the setting. That you *still* don't. Until this moment, I wasn't quite sure of that. I couldn't believe he'd keep it from you. Isn't he your partner? Isn't he your friend? . . . And I couldn't believe you'd stand for it. . . . Well, it's your pants that are being kicked, not mine. If the Burning Glass——

TONY

I never used that name!

HARDLIP

Who else? . . . My dear Tony, you have no need to be frightened. Let us be very simple and then enjoy our dinner with a light heart. You said that evening — what was it? five weeks ago? — much more than it was discreet to say. But fortunately you said it to me alone in the privacy of my rooms and no harm has been done. Still, won't you look rather a

54

fool at this . . . high-up conference, if Terriford knows the setting and you don't? What are you, for God's sake — the office-boy? And in any case, you aren't quite yourself this evening. I should have supposed that I was more suitable company for you than Mary Terriford . . . or the Prime Minister.

TONY

My God, how do you know that?

HARDLIP

(*Laughing, as at a practical joke*)

Ha! That caught you. Oh, Tony! you are very much on edge!

TONY

How *can* you know? It was arranged by telephone not half an hour ago.

HARDLIP

(*Laughing again*)

High-up conference on the Burning Glass. Prime Minister at the Manor. Conclusion obvious. (*Maliciously*) It wasn't necessary to tap your telephone, I promise you. . . . Now, shall we start? I think you need a break, Tony. The great mind isn't functioning at Cabinet level. Mine will be the more amusing party. (*He picks up his evening coat and trails it from his arm.*) Come. (*As he starts towards* TONY, *his coat sweeps the chess-table.*)

TONY

Oh, Gerry, look what you've done! You've ruined their game. (*He drops on his knees and begins to put the pieces back.*)

HARDLIP

It is quite useless to attempt that. . . . Get up. It is time to go. (*As* TONY *rises, shaken and bemused,* HARDLIP *takes him by the arm and leads him towards the door.* TONY *wrenches himself free and turns.*)

TONY

It looks like a drunken orgy. Let me put them back for her.

HARDLIP

For her! For her! And in what positions may I ask? . . . Come. (*They go out.* MARY *comes in and sits at the piano.* LADY TERRIFORD *follows her and stands at the end of the piano. Neither notices that some of the chessmen are on the floor.*)

LADY TERRIFORD

So you didn't persuade Mr. Tony to stay.

MARY

No. And yet I think he wanted to. (CHRISTOPHER *enters. He halts and listens.*)

LADY TERRIFORD

There was a bad fairy at his christening.

CHRISTOPHER

Whose?

MARY

Tony's.

CHRISTOPHER

Not at his christening. His early home was as solid as a rock. It crumbled when he was a fighter pilot, which isn't a good moment.

MARY

(*To* LADY TERRIFORD)

He isn't *bad*!

LADY TERRIFORD

No. I think you are right. But he keeps bad company.

MARY

He is generous and gay and sometimes very kind . . . and brilliant — isn't he, Christopher?

CHRISTOPHER

He is also quite insanely brave.

LADY TERRIFORD

Or rash?

CHRISTOPHER

Both. You have never seen him gamble or dive a Spitfire into a squadron of bombers. I have. His trouble is that he hasn't any longer a personal life that he in the least minds losing, which either makes a saint of a man or — oh well, let it go!

LADY TERRIFORD

What he needs is to marry a good girl.

CHRISTOPHER

He did. She was killed.

LADY TERRIFORD

Killed?

CHRISTOPHER

By one of the bombers he didn't get. (MARY *begins to move across to the fireplace.*)

LADY TERRIFORD

Before the family rock crumbled?

CHRISTOPHER

Just after. She was to have been his rock.

MARY

Poor Tony. He talks to me sometimes. He shrugs his shoulders and says he's like the modern world. It's true in a way. He believes in nothing except the things he has lost. And so he rebels and frivols and makes love, and goes to parties with Mr. Hardlip, and talks——

LADY TERRIFORD

And talks?

MARY

Oh, look!

CHRISTOPHER

What?

MARY

Half the chessmen on the floor. (*She drops on her knees and begins to pick them up.*)

LADY TERRIFORD

Someone upset the table.

58

MARY

Quiet. I can remember. (*While she is putting the pieces back into their places,* CHRISTOPHER *stands behind her.*)

CHRISTOPHER

All the King's horses and all the King's men—

MARY

But I can ! I can !

Act Drop

ACT II

ACT II

Later the same night. The lamps are on, the curtains closed. A fire has been lighted. LADY TERRIFORD *is knitting, with a book on her lap.* MARY *is at the piano. The clock chimes against her music and she ceases to play.*

MARY

What was it struck?

LADY TERRIFORD

Half past.

MARY

Past what?

LADY TERRIFORD

One. They came nearly an hour late.

MARY

They have been ages in the Unit.

LADY TERRIFORD

Monty Winthrop has always liked playing with scientific toys.

MARY

If I had been Prime Minister, I should have wanted to do it the other way round. First what the thing *was*; then the effect.

LADY TERRIFORD

What concerns him is always effect. That is why he is Prime Minister. Great men don't walk patiently from A to Z. Like fleas, they jump. They have to.

MARY
(*Moving into the bay*)
Shall I let in some air ?

LADY TERRIFORD

By all means. It's a lovely night. But I'll put on a log. He likes a blaze. (*While* LADY TERRIFORD *makes up the fire,* MARY *draws back the curtains from an open window and leans out.*)

MARY
(*Turning back into the room*)
There are men outside. (LORD HENRY STRAIT *comes in Right, carrying under his arm a despatch-case of soft black leather.*) Lord Henry, who are those men ? (LORD HENRY *is about forty, smooth, distinguished and efficient. Though he is not a member of that establishment, he is very 'foreign-office' in manner. His air is that of one who belongs to a separated and infallible caste, but he is too well-bred and too clever to exhibit the arrogance of power except, later on, to* TONY, *when* TONY *is 'down'.*)

LORD HENRY

Friends, Mrs. Terriford.

MARY

You mean guards ? Did you bring them all ?

LORD HENRY

And others, I'm afraid.

MARY

In your car ? But there isn't room !

LORD HENRY

There are more cars than one.

MARY

How do you bear it ?

LORD HENRY

I ? Oh, it doesn't apply to me . . . to the same extent . . . when I'm off the leash.

MARY

But he ?

LORD HENRY

He doesn't give it a thought. One gets used to it, you know, as one does to wearing a pair of boots.

LADY TERRIFORD

Mary is thinking that in the Garden of Eden there were no boots. (*As the* PRIME MINISTER *enters with* CHRISTOPHER, *he overhears the last phrase.* CHRISTOPHER *has a foolscap folder.*)

PRIME MINISTER

'In the Garden of Eden there were no boots.' How pregnant an isolated phrase can be on condition that you don't understand it ! In my grave, I shall still be searching for the impossible context of that remark.

If you applied your mind, Monty, you would see——

No, my dear Helen, do not tell me. I shall enjoy having something to search for in my grave. Particularly if it embraces a memory of you . . . and, if I may say so, of this historic evening. For historic it is — am I right ? Now (*to* CHRISTOPHER) shall we proceed with our task ? (*To* MARY *who has offered him a low chair*) No, I'll sit upright. At this table. Then I can walk about. I always come alive in the small hours. Tiresome for my young hostess, I'm afraid. . . . Now, let us get on. (LORD HENRY *sits within close reach of him.* CHRISTOPHER *is standing.*) Machine Six. Why Six ?

Because it is the sixth distinct type of Weather Control machine since my father began. You see, sir, at the beginning——

No. That is all the answer I want. I take it there were intermediate stages — amendments, so to speak — Four A, Four B, Four C and so on ?

Many.

PRIME MINISTER

Up to what point communicated — I mean to other men of science — abroad?

CHRISTOPHER

Up to my father's death. He always communicated his results. Men of science did. My father died in 1940.

PRIME MINISTER

I remember well. An old friend. A great loss. (*This is only formal. He has no time now for any personal feeling.*) What was the last machine communicated?

CHRISTOPHER

One of series Five.

PRIME MINISTER

Not Six?

CHRISTOPHER

No, sir. I have given Six to the Dennistoun Foundation in California. No one else. They endow Weather Control. They finance this place.

PRIME MINISTER

The enemy could have stolen it from them.

CHRISTOPHER

There hasn't been time. Anyhow why should the enemy bother? Machine Six isn't a weapon. It's completely innocuous without the Burning Glass setting.

PRIME MINISTER

Machine Six, I confess, means nothing to me. I saw the flare in the Reflex Indicators. You say that on Istik Island in the Pacific the lizards roasted and the rocks split. How do I know?

CHRISTOPHER

You don't, sir, from what you have seen. I said you wouldn't. But you have seen the reports of previous experiments. (*He pulls out a map and spreads it.*) Not only from Istik but from three other Observation Posts spread about the world. There . . . and there . . . and there. And that's Istik. I'll leave copies with Lord Henry. (*He hands a file to* LORD HENRY.)

LORD HENRY

How did these reach you?

CHRISTOPHER

Air-mail. These Observation Posts themselves are uninhabited islands. Nothing there but our recording instruments. But our observers in those parts visit them regularly and report what they find — chiefly rainfall, temperatures, hours of sunshine. That gave us all we wanted on Weather Control in the ordinary way. When I got the Burning Glass settings, I cabled for special reports. They are decisive and not pleasant.

LORD HENRY

They came home by open air-mail?

68

PRIME MINISTER

Why not in cipher?

CHRISTOPHER

Because this isn't a Government show. The Terriford Trust was my father's private pidgin to start with. Then the Dennistoun Foundation produced a Research Endowment. This has never been a secret organization.

PRIME MINISTER

From to-day onward it is. . . . Henry, when we reach London, you will . . . shut all the stable doors. (*To* CHRISTOPHER) Give Lord Henry details of your staff here and your observers outside.

CHRISTOPHER

They are included there. (*The file which is already in* LORD HENRY'S *hands.*)

PRIME MINISTER

Good. Stop all communications inward or outward until new arrangements have been made. (*To* LORD HENRY) Tell Gareth to draft what is necessary. I will see the draft myself. (*He stands up, paces away, returns and hesitates.*) Well, so far, so good. (*In fact, he is only opening a new chapter in his mind, but his eyes are on* MARY *and she rises.*)

MARY

I think we are in the way.

69

PRIME MINISTER

No. Pray sit down. You already know as much as I do — that under the Burning Glass lizards roast. All life disintegrates — am I right?

CHRISTOPHER

Yes, sir.

PRIME MINISTER

It is formidable. By night as well as by day?

CHRISTOPHER

This is the night, sir.

PRIME MINISTER

So I observe.

LADY TERRIFORD

If the sun has set, I don't see how——

PRIME MINISTER

No, no, Helen, not now. Never ask a man of science questions of that kind. He wallows in them — and it makes no difference to the lizard. (*To* CHRISTOPHER) No doubt the Terriford waves bend or something of the kind. Everything bends nowadays. Am I right?

CHRISTOPHER

No, sir. Completely wrong. You see——

PRIME MINISTER
(*With a friendly hand on his shoulder*)

My Cabinet never say that. It might be better if they did.

LADY TERRIFORD

Not for them.

CHRISTOPHER

(*Bursting to explain what is so interesting to him*)

I'm sorry, sir. But *bend* isn't the right word. What really happens is——

PRIME MINISTER

Never mind. For the moment I take it as read. Now let us return to our lizards.

MARY

Prime Minister, what Christopher is trying to say is really important and interesting. Wouldn't it be intelligent to know what the Burning Glass is as well as what it does? (*The* PRIME MINISTER *is at first vexed by this interruption.*)

PRIME MINISTER

Intelligent?

MARY

I didn't mean that you——

PRIME MINISTER

(*Relenting*)

You are quite right. . . . Tell me, then, what the Burning Glass is.

MARY

Christopher must tell you.

PRIME MINISTER

(*To* MARY)

You shall tell me. I shall understand you better.

Tell me, as you would a child. But first, let me clear the air. I know something of Radio. Am I to think of the Terriford waves in the same terms?

CHRISTOPHER

Both are electro-magnetic. There the likeness ends. Radio waves are reflected back by — call it the upper atmosphere. Terriford waves are not. They——

PRIME MINISTER

Words of one syllable.

CHRISTOPHER

They *do* things *to* the upper atmosphere. . . . Go on, Mary. As to a child.

MARY

Fifty or sixty miles outside the earth is a vast layer, which isn't air and isn't space. It is called the Ionosphere or the Heaviside Layer. It contains (*she glances at* CHRISTOPHER) ionized particles? Like all atoms they are little suns with electrons buzzing round them like planets. But ionized particles are freakish. They have one electron too few. Radio waves hit them, and are reflected back to earth, but——

PRIME MINISTER

Why?

MARY

I don't know.

72

LADY TERRIFORD

What a relief it is nowadays to hear someone say :
'I don't know.'

PRIME MINISTER

Does anyone know this, Christopher ?

CHRISTOPHER

The Radio boys have their results.

PRIME MINISTER

Without knowing why ?

CHRISTOPHER

Without knowing *finally* why.

MARY

Please listen. The Terriford waves are different.
Christopher's father found that they could——

CHRISTOPHER

Might——

MARY

That they might — I think the word is 'polarize' —
they might polarize a section of the upper atmosphere
— anyhow make it into a definite pattern so that it
would act to the sun's rays as a lens.

PRIME MINISTER

That is the word I catch hold of. Lens. Go on.
Make me understand it.

MARY

When you were a little boy, sir, did you ever take a

magnifying glass and turn it in the sun until it burnt a hole in a piece of paper or set fire to a dry leaf?

PRIME MINISTER

Oh yes, I was a very destructive little boy. . . . Is that it? Is that it? Go on.

CHRISTOPHER

May I break in? My father began by studying the connexion between ionization and light. His object and mine was always Weather Control. He did succeed in forming a kind of lens but he could never get enough power: the lens was always too far from being a perfect lens: he could obtain warmth but — it isn't easy in words of one syllable.

PRIME MINISTER

Let me try. I am a democratic politician. Always use kitchen-metaphor. Everyone understands that, even under a system of universal education. . . . When your father switched on the sun, the bath-water remained, so to speak, tepid. Am I right?

CHRISTOPHER

Thank you, sir.

PRIME MINISTER

Or shall we say you had a garden hose shooting warm sunshine accurately and now you have . . . a flame-thrower? (*They do not interrupt his long pause.*) A celestial flame-thrower. . . . Apollo's Burning Glass. . . . (*He has been meditating, feeling his way. Now he sees the whole thing, and speaks with the triumphant relief of a man who has been buried alive.*) That gives us absolute mastery.

MARY

(*In a tone of despair*)

Is that how you see it?

PRIME MINISTER

How else?

MARY

Mastery in war?

PRIME MINISTER

And in peace. You must not be shocked by the idea of *commanding* peace. Talk won't serve with totalitarians. (*To* CHRISTOPHER) Now tell me. What is to prevent the enemy from arriving independently at your result?

CHRISTOPHER

Everything.

PRIME MINISTER

You refresh me. Why?

CHRISTOPHER

Because even if they got as far as Machine Six or their own version of it, they haven't the Burning Glass setting. And won't have it.

PRIME MINISTER

Might they not develop it?

CHRISTOPHER

I didn't develop it. It came. You must get this,

sir. If you set an eternal monkey at an eternal typewriter and he went on typing and typing for ever, the time would come — must come mathematically by the laws of chance — at which what appeared on his paper would be — well, shall we say a complete sonnet of Shakespeare? The chances against my arriving at the Burning Glass setting were like that.

PRIME MINISTER

You are a very modest young man. What with your monkey and your typewriter, you make it sound as if I could have hit on the thing myself. Am I right?

CHRISTOPHER

Well sir, it would need a monkey who could type. . . . Anyhow, monkeys or no monkeys, if I forgot it now, I should never reach it again. And *they* won't in a million years.

PRIME MINISTER

Who has the setting?

CHRISTOPHER

No one but myself.

LORD HENRY

Almost as important : who knows that it exists?

CHRISTOPHER

We in this room and my chief assistant, Tony Lack.

PRIME MINISTER

Where is he?

CHRISTOPHER

He's dining in London.

PRIME MINISTER

Didn't he know I was coming ? (CHRISTOPHER *and*
MARY *hesitate.*)

LADY TERRIFORD

He was told. He was asked to stay. He wouldn't
let down his host.

PRIME MINISTER

His host must have been very important or very
charming.

LADY TERRIFORD

Neither. That, I think, is why. There are people
who don't like dining with Prime Ministers ; they
prefer night clubs. Mr. Lack has that kind of . . .
defiance ? . . . Just because Mr. Hardlip, apart from his
intellect, is such a sorry little scrub——

LORD HENRY

(Coming to life violently)

Would you say that again — the name ?

LADY TERRIFORD

Hardlip.

LORD HENRY

Professor of Economics ? Tamas Domokos Hardlip ?

LADY TERRIFORD

He is known as Gerry.

77

MARY

Do you know him?

LORD HENRY

I wouldn't say that. . . . Not as a brother. Where-ever there are strings to pull one meets him — unavoid-ably. (*He scribbles on a piece of paper which he hands to the* PRIME MINISTER, *who hands it back.*)

PRIME MINISTER

Thank you. (LORD HENRY *lights a cigarette and with the same match unobtrusively burns the scrap of paper. Meanwhile the* PRIME MINISTER *continues :*) If it would need a monkey and a million years to reproduce the Burning Glass setting, I had better have a copy now. Even young men have died in the night. Where do you keep it?

CHRISTOPHER

In my memory.

PRIME MINISTER

You mean it is not written? My dear friend, write it at once. To-morrow Walter Crisp shall make contact. You shall have support at the highest level — scientific development (that's Crisp) and Gareth, security. At present, Henry, no one else. Repeat no one. When we reach London, order security on this house and this young man without delay.

LORD HENRY

In what degree?

PRIME MINISTER

Alpha Plus . . . (*He is standing behind* CHRISTOPHER, *who is at the end of the writing-table.*) Meanwhile, I will have the setting. Write, my friend. (*He puts a pen into* CHRISTOPHER'S *hand.*)

CHRISTOPHER

(*After a pause, drops the pen into pen-tray with a little clatter*)

No, sir.

PRIME MINISTER

What ?

CHRISTOPHER

I can't write it.

PRIME MINISTER

Cannot ?

CHRISTOPHER

Will not.

LORD HENRY

If what you are afraid of is security, that surely can be left to the Prime Minister.

CHRISTOPHER

I am not thinking of that. . . . And I am talking to *him.*

PRIME MINISTER

My request is an order.

CHRISTOPHER

One I ask you not to give.

PRIME MINISTER

It is given.

CHRISTOPHER

It is one you cannot enforce. You can search me and this place. Not my mind.

LORD HENRY

To whom will you give the setting? To Crisp?

CHRISTOPHER

To no one — at present.

LORD HENRY

But that is an intolerable position. Is it a question of price? (*On that*, CHRISTOPHER *swings round at him*.)

CHRISTOPHER

My God, you can't say that. You . . . (*He stifles himself and out of the momentary silence* MARY *says very quietly*:)

MARY

Lord Henry, you know it is not true.

PRIME MINISTER

In this country we do not force men's minds. That, with all our faults, is the distinction between ourselves and the evil we resist. The issue before the world is precisely that — the liberties of the mind, the sanctity and independence of the spirit. That is why I ask where I cannot compel. I ask this power. Your own conscience must yield it.

CHRISTOPHER

Isn't it true that many who were working on the atomic bomb prayed that some principle might emerge which should make the thing for ever and ever impossible ?

PRIME MINISTER

That is true.

CHRISTOPHER

Were they right or wrong ?

PRIME MINISTER

They were right in hoping that Providence would refuse them that gross power. But Providence did not refuse it to them — or to you. The problem stands.

CHRISTOPHER

I am not shirking it. I didn't bring you here, sir, on a fool's errand. (*And now he is struggling.*) My mother has one text by which she rules her life. It was my father's too. It's in my bones. 'Render—' (*His voice breaks.*) I can't easily say it.

LADY TERRIFORD

'Render therefore unto Caesar the things which are Caesar's ; and unto God the things that are God's.' It's plain common sense.

MARY
(*Ingenuously*)

You are Caesar.

PRIME MINISTER
(*With a smile at her prompting*)

Thank you, my dear. But what would the Opposition say to that ? . . .

CHRISTOPHER

God knows I am with you on the Liberties of the Mind. They are threatened — cold and hot. They have to be protected. You had to know that the Burning Glass exists. Now, there is no threat you can't defy. In supreme emergency — and you shall be judge of that — the *use* of it is yours. But not now. And never the setting itself. Except in supreme military emergency, the Burning Glass shall not be put to use at all.

PRIME MINISTER

Not even to beneficent use?

CHRISTOPHER

Not even to what you call beneficent use. The word begs the whole question. Suppose we could harness the Burning Glass, as we are trying to harness atomic energy. Suppose we could switch on the sun to drive all our engines for us, and boil the bath-water, and grow our food and can it, and play our music and can that, and incubate our babies and can them; suppose this huge power over Nature were really on tap in every suburb from Purley to Peru — what then? There can be a blasphemy of applied science. We have reached that point. For five generations man has developed his power over Nature——

PRIME MINISTER

Is that wrong?

CHRISTOPHER

Alone it is. We haven't developed at the same time our spiritual or our political qualities. We are neither

gentler nor wiser than we were. We are like a monstrous
giant, one of whose arms has grown and grown——

PRIME MINISTER

Stop. I am not expressing an opinion, but I want to
grasp the significance of this. Do I understand that
now, for the first time, science is withholding knowledge?

CHRISTOPHER

Now, for the first time, science is withholding power.

PRIME MINISTER

Is not that reaction?

CHRISTOPHER

No, sir, it is revolution. It is revolution against the
drug that has been . . . swelling us.

PRIME MINISTER

Power over Nature is a godlike drug.

CHRISTOPHER

It happens that we aren't gods.

PRIME MINISTER

You are holding back the clock.

CHRISTOPHER

I am refusing to put it forward. To do either is to lie.
(*This is not without effect on the* PRIME MINISTER, *but the
immediacies are what concern him.*)

PRIME MINISTER

So be it. . . . For the moment, leave the civil uses ; that is long-term, anyway. Come back to the urgent, the military. If I am not to have the setting, how am I to obtain the use ? What action do you propose ?

CHRISTOPHER

I will work with your scientific advisers on Machine Six. I will work on their lines. But it is I who will set the machine.

PRIME MINISTER

And if, when emergency does arise, you are dead or absent ?

CHRISTOPHER

That has been provided for.

LORD HENRY

Then you have confided the setting to someone ? To Mr. Lack, for example ?

CHRISTOPHER

You are too quick. I said 'to no one' and I mean it. Half the setting is deeply planted in my wife's memory. That half alone is useless in itself ; anyhow she hasn't a notion of how to apply it. The other half is in a sealed and addressed envelope in the hands of a friend, a village doctor. He doesn't know what the envelope contains and would be no wiser if he did. In emergency, if I am absent, Mary will telephone to him and give him a code word. He will post the letter. The two parts of the setting will come together.

LORD HENRY

In whose hands?

CHRISTOPHER

For the Prime Minister's use.

LORD HENRY

Through what intermediary?

PRIME MINISTER

Do not press, Henry. When the kingdoms of the world are offered to me, I can wait a little while to learn the name of the intermediary.

MARY

You said 'the kingdoms of the world'. Remembering the context?

PRIME MINISTER

(*With a snap*)

I know my Bible.

MARY

The reply was: 'Get thee behind me, Satan.'

PRIME MINISTER

But I am only Caesar. Did you not tell me so? It is hard for Caesar to make that reply. . . . And who offered me the kingdoms . . . and the republics?

MARY

(*A cry of despair, rare in her*)

I wish we were peasants! I wish we had lived and

85

died a thousand years ago ! Even the choice between good and evil seems to have been taken from us.

PRIME MINISTER

It has not. That is despair. So the entanglements of the world always appear in our darkest hours. It seems then that we cannot stretch out a hand without wounding, or speak without denying, or kiss without betraying. The pieces of silver burn in our palm and the cock crows in our ears. The words of the Gospel itself seem to conflict with one another, good fighting against good, and we call it the modern dilemma and pity ourselves. But it is the dilemma of the two sisters, the one who served and the other who sat at Jesus' feet. It is the dilemma of Pilate, who also was a minister of Caesar : at least I have learned that we cannot wash our hands of it. What we call contradiction is often, without our knowing it, the perfect balance of truth itself. The contradictions in the words of Jesus are all a seeming that we shall grow out of ; to underline them with our intellect is pride ; to use them as an excuse for inaction is cowardice. We are to choose fearlessly. To-night you and your husband have chosen. Your conscience was divided against itself, a part saying : 'Render unto Caesar,' and a part : 'Resist not evil.' And you have chosen ; that is much. Do you now blame yourself that you seem to have sacrificed a part of your conscience ? I have come to believe that this is a sacrifice often required of us while we live — our acknowledgement that our conscience is not infallible. Let no man call himself an idealist who has never sacrificed an ideal. (*He has been so carried away by his own thought that he has not noticed that* LORD HENRY *is writing. Now he does.*) What are you writing?

LORD HENRY

Your last sentence. 'Let no man call himself an idealist who has never sacrificed an ideal.' I thought that it might be politically useful.

PRIME MINISTER
(*Sharply*)

You are too clever. (*Then with a laugh*) Either you are too old, or I am too young for this wicked world. Before I return to London I want to say this, particularly to you (MARY) if I may. If it should become known that this power exists, your Christopher may be in some danger.

MARY

I understand that.

PRIME MINISTER

Government can only help those who help themselves. You will find at first that to be protected is irksome, but it is really no more than a return to one's nursery days. One gets used to it and forgets it. In effect, I myself never go out except in a pram. Fortunately, a tolerably invisible pram. But you two must not think it clever or amusing to give your nursemaids the slip.

MARY

We shall not do that.

PRIME MINISTER

Very well. From to-morrow———

MARY

I want to ask you something. Will you stay here to-night?

LORD HENRY

That is impossible.

MARY

I suppose it is.

PRIME MINISTER

But I am interested.

LORD HENRY

I'm sorry, sir. It is completely out of the question.

PRIME MINISTER

I am aware of that. Permit me, nevertheless, to be interested. (*To* MARY) What is it you fear?

MARY

I don't know. If I did, I should not fear it.

CHRISTOPHER

My darling, there is nothing to fear. How can there be to-night? Tell me.

MARY

Very well. Say no more. There is nothing to fear.

PRIME MINISTER

When I am gone, what shall you do?

MARY

Play chess with Christopher. It's our bedtime peace-and-quiet. More than ever now.

PRIME MINISTER

And you, Helen?

LADY TERRIFORD

I? Sit here and read or knit.

CHRISTOPHER

It's long after your bedtime.

LADY TERRIFORD

There are nights on which one prefers company.

PRIME MINISTER

(*To* MARY)

Listen, my dear. I feel no present alarm. If they knew of this thing, they could have struck before now; you lay wide open. It's the future we have to worry about, and protection will be adequate as soon as it can be laid on. Nevertheless, I want you and Christopher to know that, at all times, as if I *were* here, you can have at once counsel and help at the highest level. (*To* LORD HENRY) Give them access.

LORD HENRY

May I say, sir, that I think that goes beyond the needs of the case. Gareth's line should be enough.

PRIME MINISTER

Give them personal access.

LORD HENRY

Very well. In extreme need you telephone Whitehall 5422. When they answer, you will say: Seventeen Eighty Five. They will repeat: Seventeen Eighty Five and you will correct them: One Seven Eight Niner. When they reply, you will say one word: Flashlight.

PRIME MINISTER

I said *personal* access.

LORD HENRY

So be it. When One Seven Eight Nine replies, you will say one word: Curtain-raiser. It gives you instant access by day and night to the Prime Minister himself if he is reachable; if he is not, then still to over-riding authority. . . . Curtain-raiser is not to be used unless the heavens fall.

CHRISTOPHER

It shall not be.

PRIME MINISTER

Then I will say good-night. (*To* CHRISTOPHER) We understand each other, I think? No man has wielded so great a power with so little ambition. I live and learn. (*To* MARY) Sleep well. Sleep safe. God keep you all. (*To* LADY TERRIFORD) Good night, dear Helen. (*She walks to the door with him.*) Good night. (*He kisses her.*) Some day, you and I will go up the Cher again in a punt and attend the Commem. Ball at — where was it? — New College or Worcester?

LADY TERRIFORD

Both, Monty, I'm afraid. . . . And now will you let

me tell you why in the Garden of Eden there were no
boots?

PRIME MINISTER

Certainly not. I like puzzles and shall hereafter. It's
a long time I shall have to spend in Westminster Abbey.
(LORD HENRY *has by this time said all his farewells and he
goes out with the* PRIME MINISTER. CHRISTOPHER *follows
to see them off.*)

MARY

What happened at New College?

LADY TERRIFORD

We danced, my dear.

MARY

And at Worcester?

LADY TERRIFORD

At Worcester we more frequently sat out. There are
no pleasanter gardens in Oxford.

MARY

I believe, if I had been proposed to by a Prime
Minister, I should say so forty years on.

LADY TERRIFORD

For that two things would be necessary; first, to break
the rules; secondly, to be proposed to by a Prime
Minister. I hope neither will happen to you.

MARY
(*Embracing her*)
What a pity that so charming a woman should have

been so well brought up ! (CHRISTOPHER *returns. Sound of departing motor-cars.*)

CHRISTOPHER

There they go. Listen. Really, it's like a circus. Do you think that from now onwards when I go down to the sea to bathe or into the village for an ounce of tobacco I shall have to go in *three* motor-cars ? . . . Now, Mary, shall we play our game ?

LADY TERRIFORD

Chess ? Now ?

CHRISTOPHER

Why not ?

LADY TERRIFORD

Because it's to-morrow morning.

CHRISTOPHER

You show no sign of going.

LADY TERRIFORD

But I am old. Like the Prime Minister, I come alive in the small hours. Mary must be tired.

MARY

How soon will they lay on this . . . 'security' ? How long have we ?

CHRISTOPHER

What do you mean ?

MARY

How long before the — before the key turns in the

lock ? When it does, we shall never be just ourselves again. There will be guards everywhere. (*There now becomes audible the distant sound of a helicopter landing.* LADY TERRIFORD *hears it — an alert straightening of her body while still seated.*)

LADY TERRIFORD

But you yourself asked the Prime Minister to stay !

MARY

I know.

LADY TERRIFORD

With his guard ? (LADY TERRIFORD *rises, listens and goes to the window. The sound of the helicopter is distinct to the audience, though* MARY *and* CHRISTOPHER *disregard it, and it does not cease until 'Better than my dull chess'.*)

MARY

I know. That was one thing. But he didn't. And so that's another, isn't it ? — a kind of . . . reprieve ? So let's not waste it. I never wanted to *sleep* at the end of the holidays.

CHRISTOPHER

(*Tenderly and playfully because she is on edge*)

My darling, what did you want to do ? Shall we . . . shall we take the car and drive to the sea and swim ? It may be September but the water is still warm. Shall we ? (*And he adds, out of consideration for her:*) Better than my dull chess. (*The sound of the helicopter stops.* LADY TERRIFORD *turns from window, looks at them and comes downstage. She is behind* CHRISTOPHER'S *chair at 'Venomous. I remember'.*)

93

MARY

Nothing is better than *our* dull chess. I never wanted — I mean at the end of the holidays — people used to invent 'special treats'. They made it worse. I wanted everything to go on quite naturally — I do now — as if it weren't the end. (CHRISTOPHER *has seated himself at the chess-table during this speech.*)

CHRISTOPHER

Then we'll play. Whose move?

MARY

Yours. I had moved my pawn — that one.

CHRISTOPHER
(*Sits*)

Venomous. I remember. (*Pause.*) Mother, your job is to knit or read, not to walk about. (*She is standing near him. With his eyes still on the chess-board, he reaches up an affectionate hand which she takes and holds.*) Why did you say what you did to the High Command — about preferring company to-night?

LADY TERRIFORD

There are nights, aren't there — there were in Scotland when I was a girl — on which one expects the door to open?

CHRISTOPHER
(*Pressing her hand against his cheek*)
What does one do then?

LADY TERRIFORD

One knits — facing the door. (*She moves away and sits down on the single-ended sofa facing towards the door Left.* MARY *watches her and does not notice that* CHRISTOPHER *has moved a chessman. He recalls her by tapping with it on the board.*)

CHRISTOPHER

Mary, I have moved. Where have you gone to? (MARY *looks over her shoulder at the door Left, which* LADY TERRIFORD *is facing. Then turns back.*)

MARY

Give me the doctor's number and the code-word.

CHRISTOPHER

To-morrow.

MARY

To-night.

CHRISTOPHER

When we have finished our game.

MARY

Please : now.

CHRISTOPHER

My dearest, why on earth ?

MARY

Please : now.

CHRISTOPHER

Of course. (*He writes and gives it.*)

MARY

Bless you. . . . Now we will keep our minds on the game. (*She moves a piece quickly and decisively. He moves at once. She raises her hand, then draws it back.*)

MARY

(*To herself*)

Steady! (*She pauses to think; then moves a piece.*) I mustn't be rattled. I . . . must *not* . . . be rattled.

CHRISTOPHER

You talked as if——

MARY

What?

CHRISTOPHER

As if a wolf had his paw under the door.

MARY

(*Reaching for his hand across the table*)

Go away, wolf.

CHRISTOPHER

(*Not turning*)

Has he gone, Mamma?

LADY TERRIFORD

No. (*She rises. A car is heard. No one speaks. The car sweeps past the open window. The sound dies and stops as the car rounds the end of the house.*)

CHRISTOPHER

Tony. I'll go and let him in.

MARY

He has his own key.

LADY TERRIFORD

In any case he may prefer to zigzag quietly to bed.

CHRISTOPHER

You are unjust, Mamma. It lights up his brain and his hands — never his legs. It makes him more alive, not less. (HARDLIP *comes in, supporting* TONY *by the arm.* TONY *is very pale and almost spent, but he is not drunk and bitterly resents* HARDLIP'S *repeated suggestions that he is. He has been doped but does not know it. The effect upon him is that he is swept by waves of almost irresistible sleepiness, and he fights against them, talking in the intervals with keyed-up speed and lucidity.*)

TONY

I don't need your arm. I am not in the least drunk. Why do you pretend that I am? Only to make Mary hate and despise me.

HARDLIP

(*With the exasperating patronage of a nursemaid*)
Of course you're not. Only a little tired. (*To the others:*) I'm sorry to butt in at this time of night, but I thought it best to bring him in and make sure he got his head down safely.

MARY

Thank you. We will look after him if he needs looking after. (TONY *is seated on the sofa and, in spite of his efforts, his head continually falls forward.*)

CHRISTOPHER
(*Going to him*)
What's wrong, Tony?

HARDLIP
Poor chap. . . . Coming out into the fresh air and then the drive down. He wouldn't let himself pass out. Better if he had. Anyhow, what matters is to get him to bed. Shall we do it together?

TONY
(*Wrenching himself up from the sofa*)
I wish you wouldn't stand over me and talk as if you were visiting my grave in a churchyard. (*He seats himself on the sofa arm and speaks with extraordinary eagerness and relief.*) We stopped at the roadside——

HARDLIP
Engines hot.

TONY
I know. I didn't pass out. And then cars swept past. Car after car after car. Dozens. Like a circus. And then we came on. I know. I am alive. Very, very sleepy, but alive, all right. So are you all, sitting here. Oh, I'm glad. I'm glad. I don't know why I should be. . . . Knitting. Mary at the chess-table. (*To* CHRISTOPHER) Why aren't you?

CHRISTOPHER
I was. It's my move.

TONY

Peaceful, silent game. I ought to play it. Used to once. . . . Fire burning, lights up ; you all peacefully here. I had an idea that the room would be dark and empty and cold. . . . You know how it is after a party. Sometimes, at the very end, one wants company. . . . How long has the——

HARDLIP

He was going to ask : how long has the Prime Minister been gone ?

CHRISTOPHER

Well on his way by now.

TONY

I hope he finds someone sitting up by a fire with the lights on. (*His hands to his head.*) You know it is extremely odd. I'm perfectly alive and bright, but about once in five minutes sleep hits me on the head like a revolving sledge-hammer. It did in the car. If I'd gone under I should have stayed under, and Gerry would have brought me in like a sodden stiff — much to his satisfaction. And now . . . if I let . . . let go, I shall . . . just . . . fall on the ground and sleep . . . on the carpet. So I won't. Good night, Lady T. Give me credit : at least I go to bed under my own steam. Up those stairs. Up and up. Angels and ministers of grace defend us. (TONY *goes out.*)

LADY TERRIFORD

He has what he would call 'guts'. He deserves to sleep well.

I

CHRISTOPHER

(*To* HARDLIP)

Will you have a drink for the road?

HARDLIP

Thank you, nothing. I hope I'm forgiven for interrupting your game? Will you see me safely off the premises? You'll want to lock up.

LADY TERRIFORD

You go on with your chess, Christopher. I will see Mr. Hardlip out.

HARDLIP

(*Disconcerted by this*)

That would be——

LADY TERRIFORD

Not at all. A pleasure. (*As she goes, he has to follow her.*)

CHRISTOPHER

You know, Mary, Tony is *not* drunk.

MARY

Then what? He showed me once a little glass tube that he always carried — since the last war, I believe. Small tablets, five of them. He said that, if you were in a room, it was as well to be sure that the window opened.

CHRISTOPHER

I know his 'window-opener'. Enough to kill him twice — and to spare. Whatever he has had to-night, it isn't his own little glass tube. That has a delayed action, but minutes, not hours.

MARY

Still, go and see if he's all right. (LADY TERRIFORD *returns.*)

CHRISTOPHER

I will. I'll make this move first.

MARY

But you haven't thought about it.

CHRISTOPHER

Oh yes, indeed I have. If you allow yourself to be interrupted by the Hardlips of this world, you become (*he moves a piece*) as mad as they are.

MARY

(*Moving a piece at once*)
Now what do you do ?

CHRISTOPHER

Have a look at Tony. Then I'll come back.

MARY

Would you rather stop ?

CHRISTOPHER

No. We finish that game before we sleep. It's a thing. (*Sound of knocking at the window.* CHRISTOPHER opens it. HARDLIP *leans in.*)

HARDLIP

It seems to be my fate to interrupt you to-night. My infernal self-starter has packed up. Would you give me a turn on the handle? I'm no good with this arm of mine.

CHRISTOPHER

I'll come. (*Moves towards door Left, then turns back.*) Easier through the garden if the front door is bolted and chained. (*He opens the long window.*)

HARDLIP

Good night again. (*Vanishes.*)

CHRISTOPHER

(*At the long window*)

You can play for me if you like. Knight to King's Bishop Two. (*Goes out.*)

MARY

You had better take time to think about that one. (*There is a period of waiting, occupied at considerable intervals by these fragments which are not part of a continuous conversation.*)

LADY TERRIFORD

His car wasn't *at* the door. It was across the drive under the big elm.

MARY

Turned ready to start, I suppose. (*She sits at the piano, strikes two or three chords, then is silent.*)

LADY TERRIFORD

Yes, play. . . .

MARY

Matthew, Mark, Luke and John
Bless the bed that I lie on. '

LADY TERRIFORD

Did you too have that in your nursery ?

MARY

Christopher did.

LADY TERRIFORD

Ah ! Ah ! You were saying it for *him*.

MARY

He is taking a long time.

LADY TERRIFORD

They had to go round the end of the house. . . .
Have you ever known a machine that worked ?

MARY

A piano is a machine.

LADY TERRIFORD

Yes, play.

MARY

At New College or in Worcester gardens, what did
you hear in the very small hours of the morning ? (*She
begins the* Songe d'Automne, *then stops in mid-bar and
rises, listening. The car sweeps past the window. The
sound dies away.*)

LADY TERRIFORD

Go back to your chess-table, my dear. He will come. (MARY *remains quite still, listening.*)

MARY

He doesn't come.

LADY TERRIFORD

He will now.

MARY

I was foolish to-night, asking the Prime Minister to stay. I suddenly saw myself standing here like this and saying: 'He doesn't come', and you said: 'He will now.' . . . I am going to look. (*She goes to the long window.*) Christopher! (*She goes out.*) Christopher! Where are you? Where are you? (*Her calling dies away. Silence.* LADY TERRIFORD *rises, looks straight out at the audience in profound hesitation. Her hand goes to the telephone receiver, and lies on it ; then lifts it ; then replaces it.*)

LADY TERRIFORD

Not yet. (MARY *re-enters.*)

MARY

He isn't there. He is gone.

LADY TERRIFORD

Quiet, my dear. There may be simple explanations of everything. Give him a little time. He may have gone into the lower garden. Or he may have — that *is* possible — he may have gone straight up to Tony Lack.

(TONY *enters Right. He has taken off his coat and waistcoat and shoes and undone his collar. Apart from that, he is still in crumpled evening dress. His hair wild, his eyes staring.*)

TONY

What has happened ? Where is he ?

MARY

Has Christopher been with you ?

TONY

No.

MARY

Then who woke you ? Why are you here ?

TONY

God knows. I was — oh, deeper than sleep, on the bed of the ocean ; and something came with all its hands and dragged me up . . . and up . . . as though I were . . . necessary . . . up here.

MARY

He has gone, Tony. Hardlip came back to that window. His self-starter wouldn't work. Christopher went to help him because he was alone and has a withered hand.

TONY

Hardlip wasn't alone . . . I tell you he was not. He always keeps his toadies waiting. There were two men in that car.

LADY TERRIFORD

I didn't go out to the car itself. It was under the big

elm. (*She picks up the receiver and hands it to* MARY.) Do not hesitate. Act. (MARY *dials for the local exchange and listens. This little scene between two disciplined women is played with tense and deadly calm.*)

MARY

Exchange. This is Lamberton 46. I want London, Whitehall 5422. It is very urgent, please. (*Pause.*)

LADY TERRIFORD

From here to the Cabinet Offices the line is open. Speak cautiously, Mary.

MARY
(*Covering the mouthpiece*)

The Prime Minister isn't in London yet. They may not listen to me.

LADY TERRIFORD

If you use the word he gave you, it will open their ears. (*And now the London call comes through.*)

MARY

Cabinet Offices? . . . Seventeen Eighty Five. . . . No: One Seven Eight Niner. . . . Curtain-raiser.

Act Drop

ACT III

ACT III

Scene 1

Six days later. Sunday. Late dusk. LADY TERRIFORD *is discovered.* LORD HENRY *enters with papers that he lays on the writing-desk. On this desk there is now a green telephone in addition to the other two.*

LORD HENRY

The Prime Minister is on his way from the Manor. I'm afraid he asks once more that he may have the use of this room.

LADY TERRIFORD

He shall. Though why for six days he should have picked on this room of all others in the house——

LORD HENRY

Blame me. (*Touching the green telephone*) This link with his own secure line from the Manor to Whitehall had to be laid on. Quickest from this room.

LADY TERRIFORD

So be it. . . . At what time is the final stroke?

LORD HENRY

Soon now. We said 'at nightfall' — to-day, Sunday, if your son was not in our hands by then. We have

109

given every kind of facility for his return. New guarantees were delivered last night — not of course through diplomatic channels. In reply, not a move or a word.

LADY TERRIFORD

So now we are at the end.

LORD HENRY

(*Always with heartless efficiency*)

Everything that can be done, has been. The two preliminary strokes on Wednesday and Friday ought to have made the enemy see reason. They were precisely located in advance and timed by local time. They were carried out with perfect accuracy. That we know. There is a neat hole four miles across in the Laderek forest, and on Friday the Sumahdin Lake in effect boiled over. The enemy have been left in no doubt that we can strike where we please and when. But they have said nothing.

LADY TERRIFORD

I should have thought that made the final stroke at their capital . . . meaningless. The Prime Minister will go forward ?

LORD HENRY

I leave you to judge his mind.

LADY TERRIFORD

War won't bring my son back if the threat and two demonstrations — the forest and the lake — have failed.

LORD HENRY

It's natural you should see it from that point of view,

Lady Terriford. Believe me, our whole object has been
to get him back. Now . . .

LADY TERRIFORD

You abandon him.

LORD HENRY

I was going to say : We can't have him there and
wait. If his knowledge remains in their reach, it becomes
imperative to strike first.

LADY TERRIFORD

Did the Prime Minister ask you to explain this to me ?

LORD HENRY

Not in so many words. (*The green telephone rings.*)
Henry Strait. (*Listens.*) No. I will not even tell him.
(*While he talks,* LADY TERRIFORD *goes out.*) The story is
clear. He is staying at the Manor, but will preside at
to-morrow's Cabinet in London. (*The* PRIME MINISTER
enters.) Meanwhile, he will take no calls except Curtain-
raiser and, of course, the Palace.

PRIME MINISTER

Who is that ?

LORD HENRY

Joan.

PRIME MINISTER

More boxes ? She says I'm neglecting them, poor
girl. They will have answered themselves by to-morrow
morning. . . . You know, Henry, it's clever of the
enemy not to answer ; the one thing I didn't expect.

111

No denial of having taken him. Laderek and Sumahdin, two acts of war ; and not a protest. Not a word in their press — or even in ours. Five days of complete silence and the diplomatic patter going on all the time. Do you know why ?

LORD HENRY

No, sir, I don't.

PRIME MINISTER

Nor do I. . . . Still no reply from Washington ?

LORD HENRY

There's a stream from Washington.

PRIME MINISTER

I mean about Machine Six. I must know what likelihood there is that the enemy have Machine Six. If they pinched it from America and Christopher can be made to talk. . . . It is vital to know. As it is . . . I have to guess. And I have to guess right. . . . I observe two things. One : the enemy doesn't answer. Two : he doesn't bomb this place.

LORD HENRY

That would mean war. Maybe he's not ready.

PRIME MINISTER

From his point of view, better a premature war with existing weapons. I should have supposed he'd risk anything to bomb Machine Six. (*The door Right opens and* TONY *comes in. Throughout the following scene* LORD HENRY, *being morally a little man, is vindictive towards*

TONY, *while the* PRIME MINISTER *gives him room to breathe
— and talk.*)

LORD HENRY

Not yet, Mr. Lack.

TONY

(*Standing his ground*)

I have something to say which you must know,
(*commandingly*) and at once.

PRIME MINISTER

Come in. What I want to know is the mind of the
enemy. Can you prompt me in that?

TONY

I may. I don't know. That's for you to judge. I
have tried to tell you all I know — what happened
before, and what happened that night when he drugged
me. At the restaurant he had telephone calls. On the
road, close here, we lay by until your circus went
through. Then, in this room, when Christopher *didn't*
see him out, he must have thought damned fast. That
pretty game with the self-starter — that was a quick one.
What puzzles me is how he had a helicopter on tap.

LORD HENRY

It needn't puzzle you.

TONY

Why not?

LORD HENRY

Because it's none of your business.

PRIME MINISTER

(*Covering* LORD HENRY'S *ill-temper*)

In fact, as we now know, he had had it at close call for nearly five weeks. He moved it in to Lamberton Common when he decided to act. Lady Terriford tells me now she heard it. Presumably they were reluctant to use that method if they could get him to walk into their parlour. What changed their mind——

TONY

What made Hardlip act when he did was his know-ledge that you were coming that night and security would clamp down next morning. Then or never, if they wanted Christopher with his secret inside him and before your experts had a chance to get the hang of it. I take it our telephone was tapped. Anyhow Hardlip knew you were coming. But he knew it on his own — not through me.

LORD HENRY

We have only your word for it.

TONY

If you will believe nothing, you will learn nothing.

LORD HENRY

You had better understand, Mr. Lack, that at the moment your innocence or guilt doesn't interest us. You are not on trial in this room now. Your excuses can keep.

PRIME MINISTER

(*Impatient of* LORD HENRY)

Go on, Mr. Lack.

TONY

What I *am* responsible for is this : up to that evening Hardlip thought he had time enough. Hence the five weeks with the helicopter standing by. I had told him that I myself didn't know the Burning Glass setting. It — oh well, I can say it now — it hurt my pride not to be told, and I suppose I moaned about it. Hardlip built on that ; if I didn't know, he could be pretty sure no one else did. And out of that there's a new point which I haven't told you and which——

LORD HENRY

Really, Mr. Lack, wouldn't it have been better at the beginning to have made a clean breast of the whole thing ?

TONY

I have tried to. I am trying——

LORD HENRY

And yet you come here now and say there is something that, all this time, you have been keeping back ?

PRIME MINISTER

Patience, patience !

LORD HENRY

No doubt he is trying to work his passage home.

PRIME MINISTER
(*Angrily*)

If not patience, then for God's sake imagination ! When a man is telling the truth with all his might and all

his heart and all his soul, can't you hear it in his voice ?
(*To* TONY) Go on, Mr. Lack.

TONY

The point is : what are the enemy thinking now ?   On
that last evening, when I began to kick, Hardlip threatened
me with how much I had already told.   It was a kind of
blackmail.   I saw I was in a trap, and I burst out at him :
'Anyhow whatever else I have told, I haven't told you
the setting because I don't know it' :   I was standing
there and he *there*, and I saw something happen in his
face.   Relief, decision, I don't know — a kind of filthy
self-satisfaction.   He said something like : 'Your hysteria
convinces me !'   The point is :   until that moment, he
had never been *quite* sure that I wasn't in the secret.
But from that moment he *was* sure.   I became just a
carcase — an excuse to get him back into this house in the
small hours. . . . And it does show you the enemy's
mind.   They took their information from him.   They
too assumed that, if they had Christopher in the bag,
they had the Burning Glass too, and that it couldn't
operate without him.   When it did, at Laderek and
Sumahdin . . . you see ?

PRIME MINISTER

It can't have been pretty for Mr. Hardlip.   He has,
presumably, by now been re-gathered to the bosom of his
somewhat variegated ancestors.   That is something : one
economist the less.

TONY

But you see what it means, sir.   It does tell why the
enemy haven't bombed this place and why they won't.

PRIME MINISTER

Does it? I should have supposed the contrary. (*To*
LORD HENRY) I want Mary Terriford to come here now.
No, not the telephone, Henry. I saw her in the ante-
room as I came through. (LORD HENRY *goes out Left and
the* PRIME MINISTER *continues.*) Put yourself in their
place. They took the risk of abducting Christopher.
Why? They believed one of two things. Either that
we hadn't the guts to use this thing or that we wouldn't
have the knowledge once Christopher was taken. Now
I give myself credit; they don't doubt my guts. Therefore, it's more than a good guess that they thought we
hadn't the knowledge. And now they find we have.
Isn't that a sound reason to destroy this place at all costs
— at all costs?

TONY

No, sir. I don't believe it is if you go a step
further—— (*But the* PRIME MINISTER, *like so many
great men, has his limitations. He is just not listening
except to his own thought and he rides* TONY *down.*)

PRIME MINISTER

Every precaution that can be taken secretly has been
taken for the protection of this place, but nothing is a
hundred per cent effective against determined concentra-
tion on a single target. We must have the American
machines to fall back on.

TONY

The enemy believe you have. (*This, which is the
whole point that* TONY *has been trying to make, doesn't sink
into the* PRIME MINISTER.)

PRIME MINISTER

(*Vaguely*)

What? (*And he turns away from* TONY *as* MARY *enters with* LORD HENRY.)

MARY

You sent for me?

PRIME MINISTER

I am sorry. I must press for what I need.

MARY

If you still want the setting, the answer is still No.

PRIME MINISTER

Do not be hasty. You stand, as you think, by your husband's principle. I honour that. But it is possible to misinterpret a principle.

MARY

It was to me that he gave the Upper Setting. Not in writing. Why do you think he gave it in that form? Not to be handed on. Twice this week I have given you the *use*. I will again to-night if you order it. He meant me to do that. But I will not give you the setting. Why do you want it, if you have the use? Isn't that enough?

PRIME MINISTER

No, it is not. For this reason—— (INSPECTOR WIGG *enters.*)

WIGG

Excuse me, my lord.

LORD HENRY

Well?

WIGG

Despatch-rider from the Manor, my lord.

LORD HENRY

Bring it in.

WIGG

It's a young woman, m'lord.

LORD HENRY

I didn't say bring her. Bring it. I want the despatch.

WIGG

She won't give it me. She's stubborn as a mob of mules. Scottish, by the sound of her. Only the Prime Minister or you, m'lord, personal.

PRIME MINISTER
(*With delight*)

Go on, Henry. It's the Curtain-raiser I'm waiting for. (LORD HENRY *goes out.*) Inspector. . . . Give that girl some tea or better.

WIGG

Very good, sir. (*Goes out.*)

PRIME MINISTER

I like stubborn security. My mother was Scottish. Thank God for the Act of Union. (LORD HENRY *returns carrying a Red Box. The Prime Minister opens it with his key and takes out a single sheet.*) One sheet. Washington isn't wasting words. . . . (*For a few moments he reads to himself, then:*) In the event of war, the President will give me personal backing, but 'the fullest information will be needed to win the support of Congress. The disappearance of one man cannot of itself justify war. The nature of the Burning Glass and the urgent peril to all our people of its falling into enemy hands must be felt, repeat felt, from coast to coast. Above all it must be clear that nothing known to Great Britain has been, is being or will be withheld from the United States.' . . . Now, Machine Six. Listen, Mary ; here is your reason. He says : 'We have in the United States four operative and three under construction. They have hitherto been regarded as Weather Control instruments and have not been given military security. For the same reason, the enemy may have been more interested in other things.' . . . *May have* !

LORD HENRY

That leaves us all guessing.

PRIME MINISTER

Then there's a passage I won't read. . . . Now, listen to this : 'As the only example of Machine Six in your country is at Terriford House which may be destroyed, it is urgent and imperative that you communicate the setting to us. Without it our machines cannot help you. It is my personal request, as ally and friend, that you communicate the setting now, repeat now. I am at a loss to understand why you have withheld it.' . . . Now, Mary. If this place is destroyed, above all if the enemy have Machine Six, it is a prime necessity that the United States should operate. I claim the setting as a right.

MARY

No one but Christopher can give it.

PRIME MINISTER

The right to use the Burning Glass in supreme emergency he gave, through me, to his country. You agree?

MARY

Yes.

PRIME MINISTER

Does not that include our allies?

MARY

You press and press. I feel like a prisoner in a foreign country with no counsel to defend me.

LORD HENRY

Answer the Prime Minister's question. Does not your husband's grant of the military use of his machine extend to our allies?

MARY

The military use — yes. But the use, the use, only the *use*! He would never allow the setting itself to go out of his keeping. Didn't he say, here in this room: 'I will give you the use, but I will set the machine myself'? Now I have set it for him and you have used it. And I will set it again and you shall use it again. I would set the American machines. But I cannot be in two places at the same time, and I must not let the setting go. . . . I know quite well that when the Burning Glass was used on Laderek and Sumahdin there was a chance that Christopher would come back, and I know that, if it is used on the enemy capital to-night, I shall never, never see him again. But if the Prime Minister orders it, I will obey. Christopher would have wished that. But I will not let the setting go.

LORD HENRY

How many people do you think would understand you? If you said: 'I will not use this power in war,' there are millions who would understand that, and would applaud you until they were bombed in their own homes. And if you said: 'I will give this power for peaceful, industrial uses — to give everyone more luxury at the cost of less effort' — they would applaud that also. But you say precisely the opposite.

MARY

Christopher said the opposite.

LORD HENRY

He would give it in war but not in peace? Why? You stand on conscience. Is not war the greatest of evils?

MARY

(*To* PRIME MINISTER)

Where is he leading me? He is leading me into a trap.

PRIME MINISTER

Let him go on. You are hearing what the world would say. He knows his world.

LORD HENRY

You will not release the setting because you fear that, once out of your hands, it would be used in peacetime for what you consider evil purposes. But is not war a great evil?

MARY

It is a great evil.

LORD HENRY

Is not war the greatest of all evils?

MARY

No.

LORD HENRY

The world would say so.

MARY

That does not make it true.

LORD HENRY

What evil is greater than war? (*Pause.*)

MARY

To corrupt life. (*Pause.*)

PRIME MINISTER
(*With a certain satisfaction*)

The trap has not closed, Henry. On that line you will never shake her.

LORD HENRY

She does not know how old the world is. It is, in fact, corrupt.

MARY

At least, his science shall not corrupt it. That is what I stand out against, whether he is alive or dead.

LORD HENRY

Go out into the streets or the cinemas or the churches. Not one in a thousand would agree with him or thank him or understand him. They are aching for comfort and the power that buys it. Science has become a gigantic dole. Renounce it? Don't you believe a word of it! You are trying to change a world that doesn't want to be born again.

MARY

Then why is it so unhappy? Why are you, who have comfort and power, so bitter?

PRIME MINISTER

Ah, you fight well!

MARY

I have need to fight. Alone, against him, against you.

PRIME MINISTER

And yet, Mary, against what I ask, you must not stand out, whether your Christopher is alive or dead. Your loyalty is not to what he said in the past but to what he would say now.

MARY

Cannot I imagine that better than you?

PRIME MINISTER

I dare to think not. . . . You are——

124

MARY

You are the Prime Minister and I am utterly alone. But I loved him. I knew him. (*In an outburst of grief :*) Oh, I said : 'I *loved* . . . I *knew* !'

PRIME MINISTER

Because you have been thinking of him as if he were dead, you are holding too close to the letter of your love and loyalty.

MARY

(*Coming near and looking into his face*) I trust you. You would not trap me ?

PRIME MINISTER

(*Moved and weighed down by this confidence*) I will not trap you. I will tell you what I believe, from my experience of men, would be the truth of his mind and will — as if he were here.

MARY

Perhaps he is listening to us.

PRIME MINISTER

I will speak as if he were. . . . You cannot go to the States. There is no time and you are needed here. Therefore, the Americans cannot be given the use of the Burning Glass except by giving them the setting. And is not the *use* of the American machines in this emergency a necessary part of the military use your Christopher granted to me ? You cannot withhold it.

MARY

O please God, help me to do right!

PRIME MINISTER

If he were here, with nightfall close at hand and that paper before him — that peremptory demand — now, repeat now — would not he give me what I — must have?

MARY

(*After a struggle*)

I think he would.

PRIME MINISTER

Give her paper and ink. (*To* TONY) You too.

TONY

No, sir.

PRIME MINISTER

'No'! By God, you will do what you're told.

TONY

Not yet. Neither she nor I. If you strike, then you can have it. You can have anything then; there will be nothing left to save. But you must wait an hour.

LORD HENRY

Must!

TONY

Must.

PRIME MINISTER

An hour, you say! What if they strike before our signal has gone? Are you mad?

TONY

They won't, sir, unless you do. You are reading their mind wrong. You asked me. You *did* ask me !

PRIME MINISTER

(*Who likes courage*)

Go on.

TONY

I began to tell you. Half-way through, Mary came in. You wouldn't listen to me. . . . Once they saw that Hardlip was wrong and that we could still operate without Christopher, what was their reaction ?

PRIME MINISTER

To return him or attack. They haven't returned him.

TONY

They won't attack. We here are all thinking of what Christopher gave and what he withheld. The enemy knew nothing of that. They assume, quite simply, that, if you have the Burning Glass, the Americans have it too. They are dead sure that the American machines are in reserve. They must climb down if you give them time.

PRIME MINISTER

They have said no word. They have him and, God knows, they may have Machine Six. The Burning Glass isn't a game at which I wait for an opponent to move. The stakes are too high, my friend.

TONY

You are wrong, sir.

PRIME MINISTER

Should I not be more wrong if they struck first?
The responsibility is mine. You will set the machine.

TONY

In that, I take your order.

PRIME MINISTER

Mary?

MARY

We will set the machine.

PRIME MINISTER

Go, then, set it. Report when set. I shall act when
nightfall is beyond doubt. Afterwards we will signal.
(*They go out, Right.*) Inform the President. The setting
will follow in . . . sixty minutes. Lay on cipher and
transmission. . . . I shall sleep for half an hour. (*He
goes out Left. Down the lawn there is a sound of voices
to which at first* LORD HENRY *pays no attention He is
agitated and pours himself a drink before sitting down at the
green telephone to carry out the* PRIME MINISTER'S *orders.
He picks up the receiver and dials two numbers. As he
waits, there are more voices and orders outside the window,
at which he cocks his ear for a moment, taking the receiver
away. Then he returns the receiver to his ear.*)

LORD HENRY

Joan. Henry Strait. No, don't talk; listen. In an
hour from now we shall have a Curtain-raiser to go to
Washington. It won't be long, as messages go; a pretty
stiff series of figure groups in a rigid pattern. Probably

the devil to cipher. Who have you at the Manor? Hold on. (INSPECTOR WIGG *has come in through the long windows. To* WIGG) What is it?

WIGG

We have a man here, m'lord, I don't like the look of.

LORD HENRY

Where?

WIGG

On the lawn there.

LORD HENRY

Under guard?

WIGG

Yes, m'lord.

LORD HENRY

He will keep. I can't be interrupted.

WIGG

Very good, m'lord. (*Goes.*)

LORD HENRY

(*On telephone*)

Joan? For the moment, forget the figure-groups. I'll ring back on that. It's only a question of clearing transmission and we have an hour. Meanwhile here's an urgent one. Take it, and have it ciphered. Don't send until confirmed. Ready? Message begins. 'Prime Minister to President. Stop. Your Curtain-raiser Twenty Three; two, three. Stop. We are acting now. Stop. The information for which you ask follows

within' — hold on, I am being interrupted again. . . .
Well, Inspector ? (INSPECTOR WIGG *has returned.*)

WIGG

I'm sorry, m'lord. I think you should see him. He's
dressed queer and he's talking very queer.

LORD HENRY

Bring him then. (WIGG *puts his head out.*)

WIGG

Bring him in. (WIGG *returns.* CHRISTOPHER *appears
in the doorway with the shadowy figures of guards behind
him.*)

WIGG

Says he owns the place. (CHRISTOPHER *enters,
pauses, sways, looks around him without appearing to notice*
LORD HENRY. *He is wearing clothes with which the enemy
has supplied him.*)

CHRISTOPHER
(*Light-headed*)

Well, I do, you know, I do ! (CHRISTOPHER *sits on
his single-ended sofa, stares, crumples and collapses.* WIGG
catches and holds him. LORD HENRY'S *telephone receiver
clicks back in to its bracket.*)

LORD HENRY

O my God ! Terriford ! (*To* WIGG) Look after him.
(*This* WIGG *is already very competently doing.*) Brandy.
(LORD HENRY *goes to the drink table.*)

WIGG

Water, my lord. (*The water is brought and* CHRISTOPHER *drinks it.*)

CHRISTOPHER
(*A great shuddering sigh, then:*)
Thank you. (*And he falls back on the cushions.*)

WIGG

He'll do, give him time.

CHRISTOPHER

Where is Mary?

LORD HENRY

In the Unit.

CHRISTOPHER

Where is Tony?

LORD HENRY

In the Unit. At the Machine.

CHRISTOPHER

Why? (MARY *comes in. She and* CHRISTOPHER *do not see each other.*)

MARY

Where is the Prime Minister? The Machine is set. (CHRISTOPHER *rouses himself and sits up, listening.*)

WIGG

Steady, sir. Take it quiet.

131   L

CHRISTOPHER

I always seem to hear her voice, but she is never there. (MARY *comes down to him but* WIGG *restrains her.*)

WIGG

Not yet, ma'am. He's a bit light-headed. Comes and goes, I think.

CHRISTOPHER

'The Machine is set.' Let me get up. That's right. A bit light-headed, that's all. Let me get up. (*He gets up and moves like a sleep-walker towards the telephone.*) The Machine ought not to be set. (*Picks up the house-telephone and dials two numbers.*) Unit? This is Mr. Terriford speaking. What do you mean? . . . Don't you know my voice? Are you . . . light-headed? Tell Mr. Lack from me to come to the Private House . . . (*He clashes the receiver down.*) . . . when he's finished his drink . . . 'The Machine is set.' I always seem to hear her voice and she is never — (*and now they are looking into each other's eyes*) she is . . . O Mary, you *are* there! Touch me. (*He slumps forward across the table, stretching out his hands to her.*)

Scene Drop

ACT III

SCENE 2

A week later. Not yet quite tea-time, but on the table tea is laid, waiting for the silver kettle to be filled from a black kettle now on the hob. The room is made cheerful by the afternoon sunshine of late September, and LADY TERRIFORD *is looking out.* CHRISTOPHER *is on the sofa where he began the First Act. He is wearing pyjamas, slippers and a very scruffy woollen dressing-gown and has a rug over his knees.*

CHRISTOPHER

Surely he can't be coming yet !

LADY TERRIFORD

To tell the truth, I wasn't looking for him.

CHRISTOPHER

For what, then ?

LADY TERRIFORD

Nothing in particular. The sun. The house-martins. The lawn. My lower garden. It is such a comfort to think that my garden is still there.

CHRISTOPHER

Sentries still ?

133

LADY TERRIFORD

I expect there always will be as long as you are here.
But, being English sentries, they keep out of sight.

CHRISTOPHER

I wish the same could be said of English Prime
Ministers. He has had a very full report. Henry Strait
and Gareth sat at my bedside for hours, with one of their
Secret Women taking it all down. What more does the
great man want?

LADY TERRIFORD

How should I know, darling? He just invited himself to tea.

CHRISTOPHER
(*Hoisting his legs off the sofa*)
Then I must change myself.

LADY TERRIFORD

I think a dressing-gown will do for a convalescent.

CHRISTOPHER

Not *this* one? (*Hopefully:*) Or will it?

LADY TERRIFORD
(*Inspecting it*)
Well, perhaps not *that* one.

CHRISTOPHER

Besides, these pyjamas. . . . I think a pair of trousers
is required for Prime Ministers. What maddens me is
that the enemy kidnapped my evening clothes. They

couldn't have needed anything less. . . . (*Standing up.*)
Heigh-ho! The trouble about being convalescent for a
week is that one begins to like it. You and the doctors
say 'shock' and 'exhaustion'. May be. I was pretty
well all in. How they got me to Mitton Wood, I haven't
an idea. I just found myself on the edge of it — like
coming round in a dentist's chair. And I walked home
somehow. But I can't think back over that day from
breakfast-time onward. I tried when Strait and Gareth
were here. It's quite useless. Everything else is clear.
The Burning Glass setting is dead clear.

LADY TERRIFORD

Mary has always prayed that you might forget it.

CHRISTOPHER

Have you noticed? No miracle is ever worked to
relieve us of responsibility. I am back where I was
unless——

LADY TERRIFORD

Unless?

CHRISTOPHER

Unless I am no longer the only person who has the
whole setting. I wish I knew.

LADY TERRIFORD

What do you mean, Christopher? That you might
have given it to the enemy under some drug or in your
sleep?

CHRISTOPHER

Oh no! Oh no! I haven't even a moment's fear or
doubt of that. It's far too long and complex to be

given unconsciously. For the same reason they didn't even try torture. They would have had to use slower ways than that. . . . Oh no! *they* haven't the setting.

LADY TERRIFORD

What do you fear, then?

CHRISTOPHER

Listen. Before Mary and Tony switched on to Laderek and Sumahdin they worked together. How did they work?

LADY TERRIFORD

They went to Machine Six. The Prime Minister had pledged himself they should not be interrupted. First, Mary says, Tony put on the Lower Setting from his paper. Then she, to avoid writing her part——

CHRISTOPHER

Why to avoid?

LADY TERRIFORD

They didn't trust Henry Strait. They thought that if ever the *whole* setting were written down together it might be . . . seized. But haven't you asked Tony about this?

CHRISTOPHER

Deliberately not.

LADY TERRIFORD

Or Mary?

CHRISTOPHER

As yet, I'd rather ask you.

LADY TERRIFORD

I think you are after a mare's nest, Christopher.

CHRISTOPHER

I hope so. That's why I'd rather ask you.

LADY TERRIFORD

At first, to avoid writing, Mary suggested she should stand beside Tony at the machine and dictate. He wouldn't have that. He thought the machine might be microphoned, and do you know, I really believe Lord Henry was quite capable of it. They wanted the setting so desperately to send to America. So instead she wrote each group on a separate scrap of paper and showed it to Tony silently and destroyed it as soon as set. When both settings were on, he made——

CHRISTOPHER

I understand. He made the normal adjustments for target — the forest or the lake — go on.

LADY TERRIFORD

Then they were ready to switch on. That was all.

CHRISTOPHER

Not quite all. Did they come away together ?

LADY TERRIFORD

She came back to report that the machine was ready.

CHRISTOPHER

(*Reflectively*)

Meanwhile Tony was alone at Machine Six.

LADY TERRIFORD

He had to be.

CHRISTOPHER

Why didn't he report by telephone instead of sending her? . . . There must have been a fair time-margin before the switch-on. Mary's groups wouldn't take long to write.

LADY TERRIFORD

I can only say that Tony worked loyally *with* her from first to last. You can't think that he——

CHRISTOPHER

I don't think. I wonder . . . Mother, would you come up and valet me a bit? At the moment I'm not good at stooping for things.

LADY TERRIFORD

It must be quite a long time since I dressed you. In those days you hadn't far to stoop. (*As they move towards the door, it opens and* MARY *and* TONY *come in. He is extremely taut.*)

TONY

Is Henry Strait coming too?

MARY

I don't know, Tony.

TONY

Is he, Lady T.?

LADY TERRIFORD

I think probably not.

138

MARY

Does it matter?

TONY

It does to me. He's like a walking criminal *dossier*, the smug little cad.

CHRISTOPHER

Calm down, Tony. No one will use anything against you.

TONY
(*Defiantly*)

No one can.

CHRISTOPHER

No one will even try. This isn't an episode that it suits anyone to shout about. The enemy will remember that the Burning Glass exists, and that will moderate their language, but who do you think is going to tell the world? (*He pauses to see if* TONY *will make any answer.*) If there's damning evidence against anyone, it's against me. You didn't leave your trousers behind. Nothing's more compromising. (CHRISTOPHER *and* LADY TERRIFORD *go out.* MARY *gives the silver kettle to* TONY.)

MARY

I won't make tea until he comes. But you might fill that.

TONY

Where, in heaven's name?

MARY

From the black one on the hob. . . . Oh, Tony, matches? I'll light the spirit lamp.

139

TONY

You and your kettle and your matches! What does it feel like to have a mind at peace? Even when Christopher was gone——

MARY

Don't go back to that.

TONY

I won't ever again. I know what you went through. I watched your face all that week. But there wasn't hell in your face. Hell isn't that kind of suffering. Hell is chaos inside oneself. . . . I'll fill this kettle. (*He fills it.*)

MARY

I am using all your matches. This thing doesn't want to light. (TONY *brings the kettle back and stands waiting until a flame rises from the wick. Meanwhile she is not looking at him.*)

TONY

I wonder if it's true.

MARY

If what is true?

TONY

What Christopher said. I wonder whether there have been other . . . little patches of time which it has been agreed to leave out of history. I suppose even secrets die in the end if no one is fool enough to keep them in writing. Here is one for you. (*He takes a piece of paper from his pocket and holds it out. The flame has taken. She puts the silver kettle over it; then looks up.*) Take it.

MARY

Your hand is shaking. It is Christopher's writing.

TONY

You know it perfectly well. It is my copy of the Lower Setting — the one I used with you at the Machine. The only copy. So I give it back. I wanted you to be sure.

MARY

Of what ?

TONY

Of me. Take it.

MARY

Why should I not be sure ? What am I to do with it ?

TONY

That would be a convenient flame. (*She holds the paper near the flame but does not light it. She is seated, he standing.*)

MARY

(*Not looking at him because she feels that something
is wrong that she does not yet understand*)
Tony, you give me this as if it were of value.

TONY

Isn't it ? It is half the Burning Glass.

MARY

Without the rest it is nothing.

TONY

(*With a shrug*)
It's all I have. I thought it proper to return it to store.

141

MARY

Why not to Christopher?

TONY

O Mary, because I'm a romantic animal, I suppose.
I thought you might give a pat to the dog who brought
you his bone. We worked together at the Machine.
I've never been happier in my life — yes, *happier*. I
know you hate me to say that. But to work with you
made me happy. And I thought it might add to your
. . . peace of mind . . . to be sure that that bit of paper
wasn't sculling about. . . . I happen to love you.

MARY

(*Rising*)

I believe that is true. . . . And yet you are lying!
The moment you said: 'The only copy', I half knew.
O Tony, you are a bad liar!

TONY

Hardlip said that; now you.

MARY

You *have* a copy.

TONY

I have not. I have not. And if I had? Alone it is
valueless. You said so.

MARY

And yet you are lying in some way I don't yet
understand.

TONY

About what? How can I be?

MARY

And yet you are.

TONY

(*And now his defences are down*)

What do I say now? This scene was to have gone quite differently. You were supposed to say: 'Thank you, Tony.' And then, with all the ridiculous simplicities of this mortal life between male and female, once I had had my hands under your shoulder-blades, and let you go, I should have felt like Sunday morning after church. And that bit of paper, because you burned it, would have burned up all my sins. And I should have been — I should have gone out as white as snow. . . . My God, don't stare at me like that as though I really were some kind of redeemable leper. I shall begin to believe you love me. I can lie to myself even about that — oh quite convincingly. That is precisely the kind of shit I am. . . . Don't you grasp even now how far it has gone? It isn't a question of *half* the Burning Glass. It is all in my mind. Your part as well. The whole setting, the whole power, all, all! . . . O Mary!

MARY

What were you going to do with it? Not give it to the enemy.

TONY

Odd, isn't it? I wasn't brought up that way.

MARY

Were you going to exploit it? In what way?

TONY

How do I know? How do *I* know? I had to *have* it, that's all.

MARY

Why?

TONY

Not to be, any longer, second in my class, which I have been all my life. . . . And I have it still, even after telling you; that's what makes me laugh. I can't hand it back, can I? If it were paper I could. But it's inside me, like my special, private, personal hell. I haven't your memory or his, but I can learn, you know. Of course I can promise not to use it, and I can believe myself and you can believe me. And I can pretend to trust myself and you can pretend. . . . I believe you would trust me. . . . You did this time. I believe you would unto seventy times seven. Even Christopher might, for your sake. But don't, Mary, never, never, never, *because* I love you, and that's true, and yet I should do it again. Listen to me whining and confessing. I used at least to be gay, but the clockwork's fallen out. Never trust a self-pitier until——

MARY

You are going mad, Tony. Can you stop?

TONY

Until he's dead. . . . (*It is between these two sentences that* TONY *resolves to kill himself and takes his glass tube from his pocket.*) I might stop if I had a drink.

MARY

Then have one. . . . Nothing is hopeless. You and

I together can tell Christopher what you have told me.
Then we shall know what to do.

TONY

You and he! It's such a damned silly trivial thing,
isn't it, to have a particular woman in one's arms. There
have been so many women, all dead, and there will be
so many more. And yet never to have had *her*, and be
cold and the worms eat you . . . it seems a waste of . . .
the ensuing spring? (*She is standing at the head of the
single-ended sofa where she was when the First Act opened.
He is above her at the drink table, pouring out whisky. She
knows what is happening when she sees it in the mirror
downstage Left, and then she lets it happen.*)

TONY

Do you know, you have never before approved of
my having a drink. I promise you: this is the last.
(*He takes into his mouth the white tablets contained in his
glass tube and swills them down.*) Soon the Prime
Minister will be here. Seems absurd to me. I'll . . .
get off your carpet while the going's good. (*Comes
down to her, puts his arm across her shoulder tentatively
as at the beginning of the First Act.*)

TONY

Good-bye, my dear.

MARY

Good-bye, Tony. (*He goes up to the long windows
and opens them. She comes downstage from the sofa-end
and sinks to the ground. He turns to speak his curtain-line,*)

but though his face is convulsed and his mouth moves, even his curtain-line is a failure. No sound comes — or very little, but the actor had better know what the curtain-line would have been.)

TONY

Better to go out of harbour under one's own steam. (*He goes out. She burns the paper, then raises herself to her knees and covers her face. The sound of a motor-car which stops. A door bangs. The car goes on. The* PRIME MINISTER *enters from the garden.* MARY, *hearing him, rises to greet him.*)

PRIME MINISTER

I sent the car on round the house. (*Taking her hand*) How is he?

MARY

Christopher?

PRIME MINISTER

Who else?

MARY
(*Under stress, disjointedly*)
He will be here. They ought to have been, I know. She is helping him change. I will make tea. (PRIME MINISTER *stoops and picks up* TONY'S *empty glass container.*)

PRIME MINISTER

This little tube on the carpet. It's glass. Someone may put his foot on it.

MARY

Thank you. I'll take it.

PRIME MINISTER

(*At the tea-table*)

Six cups?

MARY

We thought perhaps Lord Henry . . .

PRIME MINISTER

Oh no. He is at the Manor.

MARY

And I wanted . . . Tony . . . to make his peace.

PRIME MINISTER

I saw him going down over the lawn. (*Pause.*) I haven't come to bother you, Mary.

MARY

I know. It's just the fact that you are what you are . . . shakes me. I want us — Christopher and me — to be . . .

PRIME MINISTER

Among those happy beings who have no history.

MARY

No public history.

PRIME MINISTER

Ah, my dear, don't make too rigid a distinction. Christians and Prime Ministers don't belong to different species. To renounce fame and power doesn't set you apart. Surrender is not peace. We are bound by the same rules. Peace, whether of a man or of a nation, has to be paid for minute by minute, hour by hour. Keep on putting your money in the slot or the lights go out.

MARY

Money ?

PRIME MINISTER

Decision, decision, decision — the hardest of all currencies. Courage — to be blamed by cowards for being ruthless. The courage to move — and not to move. The courage to reject whatever has become valueless : our prides, our ideals — even our friends ; to let them go ; to bury the dead. We must do that — we Prime Ministers, we Christians. Isn't it true ? Life demands it : the glorious courage to receive the unknown guest ; the bitter courage to say good-bye. (CHRISTOPHER *comes in.*)

CHRISTOPHER

I'm sorry, sir. No one told me you were here.

PRIME MINISTER

No bugles were sounded. I hadn't even the consideration to come in by the front door. But where is your mother ?

CHRISTOPHER

She left me some time ago. I expected to find her here. She always goes for a walk in what she calls *her* garden before tea.

PRIME MINISTER

Then let us cultivate ours. (MARY *makes tea and gives it to them.*) I have your report of the days you spent in enemy hands, and admirable it is — factually ;

148

but what interests me always is the enemy mind. I think I understand pretty well why at that stage it wasn't convenient for them to torture you. But there's a lot more I should like to understand. What is the *feel* of the place? Is it an efficient barracks — bang, bang, click clack? Or a prison with peep-holes? Or is it, like Nazi Germany, a mixture between a perversion and a pantomime with a prima donna as the principal boy? Or is it like most revolutions, when there's nothing left to plunder: a long bleak railway-station where everyone sits and waits for the trains that never come. What does it feel like? Can you tell me that?

CHRISTOPHER
(*After a pause and speaking with intense but quiet passion*)
It feels like a loathsome prep. school.

PRIME MINISTER
Does it indeed! That is new. That should throw light — if I have the wit to see by it. . . . Lead me a little. I'm on new ground.

CHRISTOPHER
I can't lead you, sir.

PRIME MINISTER
Then I must feel my way. (*Thinking aloud, doubtfully working out the puzzle.*) An old-fashioned and vile prep. school. For the moment that suggests to me cold radiators and rancid butter. . . . What more? . . . (*And now he is on the scent.*) I see. Oh yes, I see now. . . . A prevailing spirit of muscular profanity.

A tough totalitarian prep. school with all the soccer eleven dressed up in leather-jackets and beating the little boys into shouting the old school songs. On the outside, hearty; on the sly, schoolboy-corrupt. Am I right? Baksheesh to the prefects; suck up to the masters; sneak to the matron, and lick the sixth form boots. And sing the old school songs. . . . Strictly conventional. Nothing is more conventional than a prep. school, except a revolution. Whatever isn't school custom, isn't done. Whatever isn't school jargon, isn't said. Whatever the whole school doesn't think, isn't thought, and what Master don't know isn't knowledge. Am I right? And beat the old school drum! Hurrah for the Hero of the School who shot six goals in the away match! Down with the reactionary hyena who whistled a tune of his own. . . . An eternal prep. school from which no one goes home for the holidays.

CHRISTOPHER

There are no holidays; there is no home.

PRIME MINISTER

Then answer me three questions. If these creatures should swarm out against us, is the Burning Glass available to us?

CHRISTOPHER

Yes.

PRIME MINISTER

Will you arrange, as you did before, that it shall be available in the event of your death — or absence?

CHRISTOPHER

Yes. (LADY TERRIFORD *comes in from the garden.*

When they would rise, she prevents them with a word and a gesture, and sits apart.)

PRIME MINISTER

Will you now make corresponding arrangements that if you, or this place, fails, the setting shall be available for use on Machine Six in the United States?

CHRISTOPHER

In war, yes.

PRIME MINISTER

A last question. In peace?

CHRISTOPHER

No.

PRIME MINISTER

Aren't you standing against the whole tide of modern thought?

CHRISTOPHER

Do you ask the question — or do you state it as your own belief?

PRIME MINISTER

I ask the question.

CHRISTOPHER

Against the tide of modern thought? I wonder whether even that is as true as it was. Tides turn. The Wonders of Applied Science have become much less wonderful than they were. Only half-baked minds any longer worship that particular Golden Calf. Men of science themselves do not.

PRIME MINISTER

Do they not?

CHRISTOPHER

The mediocrities, sometimes. Never, the originating minds. They have great dread of their own miracles. So have the people in their hearts. For example, supersonic speed. It gets the headlines and it gets the movies. But who for a moment believes that *that*, or atomic energy, or the Burning Glass, is anything else than a monstrous gadget? No one believes any more that these things are the salvation of the world. And they did when H. G. Wells went bicycling. That is the revolution. History moves in phases. The time may come — has come, perhaps — in which science will be seen again as what it is: a source of wisdom, not of power; like music and poetry, a reading of Nature, not her slave-driver. Isn't it possible that the whole era of Power for Power's sake is near its end? I will do nothing to prolong it — as long as the decision rests with me alone. I doubt whether it does any more. (*This last sentence, thrown in by* CHRISTOPHER *so casually, does not at once penetrate the* PRIME MINISTER'S *mind. When it does, it stings.*)

PRIME MINISTER

Say that again.

CHRISTOPHER

I said: I doubt whether the decision any longer rests with me alone.

PRIME MINISTER

Who else? (LADY TERRIFORD *and* MARY *rise.*)

CHRISTOPHER

I don't want to speak of it until I'm sure.

MARY

(*Coming down to him*)

You can, my darling.

LADY TERRIFORD

You can speak quite freely now. (*The effect is almost that the two women have spoken together. Now* LADY TERRIFORD *continues*) Tony Lack is dead. His body is being carried in from the garden.

CHRISTOPHER

(*To* MARY)

You knew this ?

MARY

He came to me and told me the truth. He had the whole setting in his mind. (*To the* PRIME MINISTER) You are not to think he was a traitor — except to himself. (*To* CHRISTOPHER) He would have given it back. But there's no way of giving back what is in the mind — except one. He took that.

LADY TERRIFORD

Here, in this room ?

MARY

With his drink ; behind my back.

PRIME MINISTER

Behind your back ?

MARY

There is a mirror . . . there. I let him go.

PRIME MINISTER

You were brave.

MARY

It was he who had the courage to say good-bye.
(CHRISTOPHER *jumps up and, seeing the tube on the table,
picks it up.*)

CHRISTOPHER

This tube? His? Poor Tony, his window-opener.
. . . (*He takes three quick and vigorous steps away ; then
turns about.*) Well, it's open now. (*He tosses the tube
on to the tray where it chinks and splinters.*) I was wrong
to distrust that man. (*The green telephone rings in the
silence. For a moment no one picks it up ; then* LADY
TERRIFORD *does. She listens and hands the receiver without
comment to the* PRIME MINISTER.)

PRIME MINISTER

I am speaking. (*Listens.*) No. (*Listens.*) No. (*He
puts the receiver down. It has been a long silence and they
still wait for him to speak.*) I will go now. I shall like
to think of . . . life in this house going on. (*He is
speaking in emotional stress and* LADY TERRIFORD *takes
his arm.*)

LADY TERRIFORD

I know, precisely, what made you say that.

PRIME MINISTER

Ah, my dear, we are both survivors, and that is a
lonely thing to be. . . . (*To* CHRISTOPHER) What shall

you do this evening when I am gone — you and she?
Shall you play chess? ... (*To* MARY:) I am trying to say
good-night (*but when she holds out her hand he turns
away*) and finding it not easy. I have an extraordinary
request to make. (*Now he faces her.*) Once before, you
asked me to spend the night in this house. May I accept
that invitation now?

LADY TERRIFORD

Dear Monty.

MARY

I wanted·to ask you. I didn't dare.

PRIME MINISTER

(*Sits rather abruptly on sofa beside* LADY TERRIFORD)
I am sorry. I think I am a little tired.

CHRISTOPHER

Would you like to go upstairs and rest. I'll send to
the Manor——

PRIME MINISTER

Not yet. ... We will go together to Tony's room
at a convenient time. Meanwhile I should like to sit here
quietly and know that I am to dine with you and sleep
where I dine. And I should like you to proceed as if I
were not here. I should like to sit with Helen quite
silently while you play chess.

MARY

You are wise. And kind.

PRIME MINISTER

My dear, it is only my selfishness. To see an evil power not exercised gives me even now a little hope for the future of the world. . . . Now tell me, what would happen if White moved his Bishop — there. Seems the obvious move, am I right ?

CHRISTOPHER

Well yes, except that it isn't White's turn.

PRIME MINISTER

What ? Bless my soul. . . . I used to play when I was a boy.

MARY

Why not still ?

PRIME MINISTER

My selfishness again. I have to wait too long for the other chap to move.

Curtain

PRINTED BY R. & R. CLARK, LTD., EDINBURGH